The Complete Guide to Growing Windowsill Plants

Everything You Need to Know Explained Simply

By Donna M. Murphy
and
Angela Wiliams Duea

THE COMPLETE GUIDE TO GROWING WINDOWSILL PLANTS: EVERYTHING YOU NEED TO KNOW EXPLAINED SIMPLY

Library of Congress Cataloging-in-Publication Data

MURPHY, DONNA MARIE, 1965-
 THE COMPLETE GUIDE TO GROWING WINDOWSILL PLANTS : EVERYTHING YOU NEED TO KNOW EXPLAINED SIMPLY / BY DONNA M. MURPHY AND ANGELA WILLIAMS DUEA.
   P. CM.
 INCLUDES BIBLIOGRAPHICAL REFERENCES AND INDEX.
 ISBN-13: 978-1-60138-346-4 (ALK. PAPER)
 ISBN-10: 1-60138-346-0 (ALK. PAPER)
 1. WINDOW GARDENING. 2. INDOOR GARDENING. 3. HOUSE PLANTS. I. WILLIAMS DUEA, ANGELA, 1966- II. TITLE.
  SB419.M9843 2010
  635.9'678--DC22
                              2010025852

Printed in the United States

PROJECT MANAGER: Shannon McCarthy • PEER REVIEWER: Marilee Griffin
INTERIOR DESIGN: Rhana Gittens • EDITORIAL ASSISTANT: Danielle Reed
PROOFREADER: Amy Moczynski • amoczynski@atlantic-pub.com
FRONT COVER DESIGNER: Meg Buchner • meg@megbuchner.com
BACK COVER DESIGNER: Jackie Miller • millerjackiej@gmail.com

Printed on Recycled Paper

We recently lost our beloved pet "Bear," who was not only our best and dearest friend but also the "Vice President of Sunshine" here at Atlantic Publishing. He did not receive a salary but worked tirelessly 24 hours a day to please his parents. Bear was a rescue dog that turned around and showered myself, my wife, Sherri, his grandparents Jean, Bob, and Nancy, and every person and animal he met (maybe not rabbits) with friendship and love. He made a lot of people smile every day.

We wanted you to know that a portion of the profits of this book will be donated to The Humane Society of the United States. *—Douglas & Sherri Brown*

The human-animal bond is as old as human history. We cherish our animal companions for their unconditional affection and acceptance. We feel a thrill when we glimpse wild creatures in their natural habitat or in our own backyard.

Unfortunately, the human-animal bond has at times been weakened. Humans have exploited some animal species to the point of extinction.

The Humane Society of the United States makes a difference in the lives of animals here at home and worldwide. The HSUS is dedicated to creating a world where our relationship with animals is guided by compassion. We seek a truly humane society in which animals are respected for their intrinsic value, and where the human-animal bond is strong.

Want to help animals? We have plenty of suggestions. Adopt a pet from a local shelter, join The Humane Society and be a part of our work to help companion animals and wildlife. You will be funding our educational, legislative, investigative and outreach projects in the U.S. and across the globe.

Or perhaps you'd like to make a memorial donation in honor of a pet, friend or relative? You can through our Kindred Spirits program. And if you'd like to contribute in a more structured way, our Planned Giving Office has suggestions about estate planning, annuities, and even gifts of stock that avoid capital gains taxes.

Maybe you have land that you would like to preserve as a lasting habitat for wildlife. Our Wildlife Land Trust can help you. Perhaps the land you want to share is a backyard— that's enough. Our Urban Wildlife Sanctuary Program will show you how to create a habitat for your wild neighbors.

So you see, it's easy to help animals. And The HSUS is here to help.

2100 L Street NW • Washington, DC 20037 • 202-452-1100
www.hsus.org

Dedication

Donna Murphy: *To my family, who is a constant source of inspiration and comic relief.*

Angela Williams Duea: *This book is dedicated to my mother Kathleen and grandmother Therese, who gave me a love of nurturing plants.*

Table of Contents

Chapter 2: Add Texture to Your Home With Foliage Plants   55

Chapter 3: Choosing Flowering Plants for a Splash of Color 101

Chapter 4: Freshen Up a Room With Fragrant Plants 127

Chapter 7: Plants Cannot Live By Soil Alone   181

Chapter 8: Container Essentials and Garden Designs   203

Chapter 9: Increasing Your Plant Collection With Propagation   229

Chapter 10: Protecting Your Plants From Pests and Diseases   241

Chapter 11: Continued Care for Your Plants   257

Conclusion   265

Appendix   267

Introduction

My first houseplant was a small ivy plant, which I kept on a windowsill. It was a cutting from the English ivy that grew around my childhood home, and it reminded me of the garden I helped my mother create. Twenty years later, I still have a cutting from that original English ivy growing in my sunny south-facing window. The ivy's pretty leaves, along with the foliage of several other plants and herbs, brighten my kitchen window.

A windowsill, the horizontal shelf or member at the bottom of a window opening, is among the best possible places to grow a plant — it provides your plants with the light they need, spruces up the look of your home from the outside, and improves the quality of the air in your home. In the wintertime, windowsill plants provide a green contrast to the cold, white world outside the window. In the summer, these plants extend your garden to the indoors. Whether you live in a studio apartment in the city or an old farmhouse in the countryside, a windowsill is a suitable location for growing some of your favorite plants.

Plants are Not Just for the Great Outdoors

Humans have been living with houseplants since the beginning of time. Archeological artifacts from the ancient Egyptians, Romans, and Greeks show paintings of potted plants in homes and atriums. People cultivated herbs indoors for year-round availability and used them for their natural medicinal and seasoning properties.

However, it was not until glass windows were widely available and homes were adequately climate controlled that it became practical to cultivate a variety of plants indoors. In fact, the popularity of decorative indoor plants did not rise dramatically until the Victorian era. No middle-class parlor was considered complete unless there were potted plants on a pedestal in the corner or on a small entryway table. At the same time, the affluent had heated and humidified greenhouses that allowed them to grow plants outside the range of normal climates or seasons. For example, they often collected and grew rare specimens like tropical orchids or cultivated strawberries and cucumbers when these plants were normally out of season.

Modern home environments now provide better climate control to successfully grow a large variety of foliage and flowering plants. Consequently, indoor gardening is no longer limited to those who can afford temperature-regulated conservatories.

A Healthy Companion for Indoors

Today we recognize the physical and psychological benefits of coexisting with plants. We understand their aesthetic importance in interior design and decorating as well as their practical use for healing our ailments and spicing up our food. Most of us were taught in high school biology that plants absorb the carbon dioxide that we exhale, converting it to the oxygen we need.

We have suspected for centuries that many plants could filter unhealthy chemicals that are predominant in newly constructed homes and office buildings. Chemicals such as formaldehyde, benzene, and ethylene are found in carpeting, processed wood flooring, siding, and paint. Because a growing percentage of the world's population spends 80 to 90 percent of their time indoors, researchers are investigating alternatives to improving indoor air quality. This research involves evaluating a variety of houseplants that have a natural ability to absorb and clear these poisons from our environments.

A 2009 Pennsylvania State University study published in the American Society of Horticultural Science's journal *HortTechnology* found that there are three specific houseplants that have the ability to significantly reduce indoor ozone. The plants of choice — the snake plant, spider plant, and golden pothos — are quite popular because of their low cost, low maintenance requirements, and now their reported ability to reduce other indoor pollutants.

Researchers continue to uncover the numerous benefits of houseplants in homes and workplaces. These benefits have included:

- Reduction in eye irritation
- Improved concentration
- Reduced stress levels
- Increased employee motivation
- Reduction in air impurities
- Increased worked productivity
- Reports of less dry skin
- Positive effects on headaches, fatigue, and hoarseness

As research continues to reveal more about the many benefits of houseplants, you should already have ample reasons to cultivate a few on your own windowsills. You have windows in your home that face different directions and offer different light, temperature, and humidity levels; this allows you to experiment with a wide variety of plants that require various growing conditions.

Ideal for Renters or Temporary Residents

In some cases, gardeners do not want to invest the time, money, and materials that growing plants requires in a place that they will only live for a short period of time. With windowsill gardening, you can still grow the plants you want without having to leave them behind when you move. You are free to put the time, effort, and money into your plants without sacrificing your garden when your lease ends. Renters who do not intend to stay in a home long term, those who move often for their jobs, or college students who move regularly can plant in containers and take their plants along with them to their next home.

Bringing your windowsill garden with you when you move is often a welcome sense of continuity during a hectic time. Right after a move, you will instantly be surrounded by all of your beautiful flowers, herb plants, and foliage plants.

Aesthetic Appeal

In addition to all of the practical reasons for growing windowsill plants, there are a large number of aesthetic ones as well. Containers come in so many shapes, sizes, and colors that they can be just as attractive and decorative as the plants themselves. Your windowsill garden can add a bit of color, elegance, or quirky style to your home.

Creating a windowsill garden also presents a challenge to your creativity. You can choose a single plant for a simple splash of color, or you can dream up a complex windowsill garden with multiple plants. Plus, there is no need to stick to standard terra-cotta pots or purchase the latest plastic ones for your windowsill plants. Almost anything can be used as a container for a plant — from an old work boot to a gallon jug that you want to reuse. People who want to live a "green" lifestyle can use recycled items as containers for planting. *See Chapter 8 for advice concerning container essentials and garden designs.*

CASE STUDY: WINDOWSILL PLANTS ARE MORE LIKE AN OBSESSION

Cynthia Amrose, president
The Gardeners of Watchung Hills
New Providence, NJ
http://gardenerswh.home.comcast.
net/~gardenerswh

"I always wanted a real home, with flowers on the windowsill." This lyric is one of my favorites from Carole King's *Tapestry* album. I have also fallen in love with Mary Engelbreit's artwork, which is characterized by colorful flowers and fanciful flowerpots drawn in every window of a cottage-style home.

When I was a child, I learned the basics of gardening from my grandmother, who lived in North Carolina. She showed me how to sow seeds, how to make cuttings from mature plants, and how to remove deadheads to stimulate growth and bushiness.

As a young adult, I learned mostly by trial and error — killing plenty of plants and ruining many wooden windowsills along the way. Frustrated with one too many dead plants and warped windowsills, I began gathering helpful information from a variety of sources, including books, websites, blogs, local garden centers, county extension centers,.the regional garden club — for which I serve as president — and Irma, my amazing "über-gardening genius" neighbor.

For all of my adult life, I have had plants on my windowsills. In fact, just for windowsill plants, I had a long, deep shelf built around all three windowed walls of my sun porch. I use this shelf year-round, especially during the cold months when I bring all of the delicate, winter-challenged garden plants inside. With these plants indoors, my sun porch becomes a private nursery and closely resembles a greenhouse, especially with the rows of gardenia cuttings getting their start under pickle jars.

Living for decades in a series of apartments, windowsill gardening was my way of bringing the outdoors inside and surrounding myself with summer colors and scents year-round. I have a long history with two particular plants. Rosie, the tree philodendron, has been with me since 1974. I also have a peace lily that has been a trusted and patient companion since 1980. Both of these plants have traveled everywhere with me over the years. They have been frozen, crushed, and sunburned several times. These enduring plants have even been lost for three days in a moving van, and they still produce new leaves every spring.

Although I feel I have an average level of knowledge about windowsill plants, I know I still have much more to learn.

What is Your Gardening Style?

If you are new to gardening or caring for houseplants, or if you have had trouble nurturing plants in the past, start by evaluating your gardening style. Knowing the way you approach gardening can be helpful when choosing plants that will thrive with the type of care you are able to offer. *The plants that are mentioned in this section are profiled in later chapters of the book.* You will have access to a variety of species to choose from that match and complement your very own gardening style.

The over-nurturer

When I first began growing houseplants, my mother sent me a cactus garden of native plants from her home in Phoenix, Arizona. My gardening style: I nurture plants to death. I check them daily, pluck off ailing leaves, and water them every time I notice dryness. Though my mother told me to watch the news and only water my cacti when it rained in Phoenix, I could not help primping my plants. They died within weeks by turning into a brown, mushy mess. My gardening style is an overly involved one, and once I chose plants that craved that kind of care, they flourished more than anything else I grew. Some of my most successful — and needy — plants have been an umbrella plant, an African violet, and a wandering Jew. I also find that my kitchen windowsill herb garden thrives when I constantly rotate the plants in the sun and prune them for dinner recipes.

The fickle gardener

Some gardeners are rather fickle, planning elaborate gardens but failing to follow through with the care those plants need. Other gardeners are well-intentioned but are too busy to remember to water their plants or move them from a corner that has grown too cold or hot. Many plants wilt under neglect, but there are some plants tough enough to weather inconsistent care. Cacti, philodendrons, pothos, the jade plant, and the cast iron plant are ideal choices. They grow exceptionally well in sunny, dry conditions.

The plant collector

Finally, there is the plant collector. Many plant collectors tend to be obsessive about one species, such as special orchids or ferns. Others are enthusiasts about a particular garden landscape or plant environment. When a collector specializes in one type of plant, he or she is usually an expert in the species' care, though someone can also develop a love for one variety and study on the proper care. Enthusiasts may not choose the most beautiful or well-formed varieties but may instead choose a new plant for the collection based on unusual features. The plant collector often chooses small or dwarf varieties of plants because a collection can easily take over a home. This is especially important to remember if you are cultivating a windowsill garden, where space is likely to be at a premium. Examples of favorite plant species for collectors include African violets, orchids, bonsai plants, ferns, and geraniums.

Traits of the successful garden

Regardless of your preferred gardening style, the key to any successful garden is effective planning and organization. Before you can have a great windowsill garden, spend some time considering the layout of the garden, the choice of plants, the season of blooms for flowering plants, and a regular maintenance routine.

To get started, decide what you want from your windowsill garden. Will it serve a practical purpose? Will the garden be maintained for aesthetic reasons? Whatever the reason may be, use the following time-saving routines to help you manage your windowsill garden effectively:

- Use a loose-leaf notebook to keep a monthly schedule of reminders for watering, fertilizing, pruning, and propagating.

- Allocate a certain amount of time, say 30 minutes, on each windowsill garden and then move to the next.

- Keep all gardening essentials — pruners, watering can, plant food, spray bottle, notebook, and gloves — in one central location.

Even though you may have never grown houseplants or planted a windowsill garden before, many of the plants in this guide are relatively easy to grow and care for. Careful planning and selecting the right plants for the right environment are important to your success.

What to Expect From This Guide

This book will guide you through the process of selecting the right plants for your windowsill and fitting them into your existing space and conditions. You will learn everything you need to know to effectively nurture windowsill plants and combine foliage, flowers, and colors to produce special effects. Detailed descriptions and lists will help you select plants that are best suited for the limited space of a windowsill and which ones will only give you problems. You will learn how much light, soil, and fertilizer each plant needs and whether you need to provide supplementation. From first planting, whether by seed or potted plant, you will have every resource you need to keep your windowsill plants alive, healthy, and thriving in their new environment.

KEY

To designate plants that are **toxic** or **air purifiers** the following symbols are used throughout the book:

 TOXIC PLANTS

 AIR PURIFIERS

Chapter 1

Things to Know Before Selecting Your Plants

Today, there are many places where you can purchase houseplants, but the quality may vary based on the seller and the price you pay. Once you purchase a plant, if you take good care of it, you may have it for the rest of your life. For that reason, it makes sense to take some time and effort at the store to pick a healthy, satisfactory houseplant that will flourish where you put it. This section provides some guidance on how to determine your home environment, where to look, and how to be a well-informed plant selector.

Photo by Angela Williams Duea

The Components of Houseplants

Understanding the parts of plants and how they work will help you to become a better indoor gardener. Your plants can be healthier, you can identify problems more easily, and you will be informed to meet the needs of each type of plant.

The root of the matter

The roots of a plant are like anchors in the soil, holding the plant in the pot so it does not fall over. Roots absorb water and minerals from the soil and store extra food for future use. The section of root that attaches to the plant above the soil is called the root crown.

Some plants have a taproot, a thick, central root that grows vertically in the pot, similar to a carrot or parsnip. Smaller roots branch off from this main root. Other plants have many fibrous roots that spread throughout the soil rather than one main root. Plants such as amaryllis, daffodils, tulips, and some types of begonias have thick, fleshy roots that store food with a small root ball at the bottom, which can be either a bulb, corm, or tuber, depending on the type of plant. Over time, many of these plants will propagate by producing additional bulbs that can be replanted in a new pot.

Plants such as strawberries, spider plants, or oregano have stems called stolons or rhizomes, both of which produce adventitious roots that spread horizontally from stems or a central spot on the plant. These roots often sprout outward from stems and attach to supporting structures or plant themselves into the soil. You can see this on the common English ivy or in mint plants, which become invasive outdoors.

From stem to stem

Stems support the plant and act like veins and arteries, transporting water and nutrients from the roots to the leaves and other plant parts. Stems attach to the roots at the plant's crown, which usually should be buried under the soil. There are different types of stems; herbaceous stems are bendable or tender, such as the stems of a spider plant. Other plants, such as jade plants or ficus, have woody, tough stems, similar to the stems of bushes or the trunk of a tree. In addition, some plants produce many stems, such as the white flag or umbrella plants, while other plants produce one stem to which all leaves and flowers are attached, such as an orchid.

Some plants develop multiple stems from one crown, while other plants produce one main stem from which smaller stems and leaves sprout. There are plants that produce young plantlets, or offsets, from the main, or "mother," plant. Stems can grow downy or prickly hairs, or in the case of a cactus, produce sharp spines. Some stems have a twining or vine-like growing habit. Once these stems find something to twist around or a support for the vine, they will begin to attach to the object. This can be damaging to other plants on your windowsill, so keep an eye out for this action.

Turning over a new leaf

The stem that connects the leaf to the plant is called a petiole. The leaves themselves have different growth habits. Some produce a burst of leaves from one petiole, while others have just one leaf per petiole. Leaves receive water and nutrients from the stem and use it to generate the photosynthesis process that makes food for the plant. Leaves have a network of veins like the capillaries in our bodies. Leaves will lean toward the best source of light. The plant will orient the upper sides of the leaves to capture sunlight and begin the photosynthesis process. Leaves also contain tiny pores called stomata, which absorb carbon dioxide and other pollutants from the environment and release oxygen. This is the reason that plants are healthy housemates — they improve quality of the air in your home.

At first glance, the arrangement of leaves on a plant might look similar, but there are actually a variety of patterns to their growth. Some plants have an alternate leaf arrangement in which the leaves are staggered along the stem with only one leaf on each petiole. Some have a symmetrical arrangement of leaves sprouting from each side of the stem. Leaves come in an amazing variety of shapes and colors, from dark green to red, and even striped or spotted. They can have long, ribbon-like shapes or scalloped edges. Some leaves to do not look like leaves — think of the shape of moss — but are still able to combine water, nutrients, chlorophyll, and sunlight to produce food.

Flowers, flowers everywhere

Plants reproduce though flowers. Flowers usually contain many parts, but they reproduce through pollen and tiny eggs called ovules. Some species produce male and female flowers and can self-pollinate. Other plants are either male or female and may require two different plants to cross-pollinate before reproduction can occur. When the flower's pollen fertilizes the ovule, the ovule develops into a fruit or seed. Note that pollen is often a dry powder that stains skin and clothing; try to avoid getting it on anything that will stain easily.

Flowers come in a profusion of shapes and colors, just like the leaves of a plant. Many houseplants are bred for their beautiful flowers, but some of these will require extra attention to keep them blooming. Some houseplants grow flowers that are almost unnoticeable but have been bred for some other characteristics, such as showy leaves. A special kind of flower is the bract, a modified leaf that has evolved into the petals of a flower but may not produce seeds or fruit. One beautiful example is the bird-of-paradise plant; the red or white leaves of a poinsettia are another example. However, once the poinsettia blooms, it is almost impossible to get it to bloom again.

Plants produce flowers to propagate themselves. They will continue to produce blooms until most have died back, assuring good pollination and fertilization. You can encourage your plants to keep blooming by removing faded flowers and providing extra nutrients during the blooming period.

Uncovering the Identity of a Plant

When you receive a cutting — a leafy part of stem from a mother plant that can be used to start a new plant — from a friend or family member, or fall in love with an unlabeled plant in a store, it may not be easy to find out what species you have and how you should care for it. Finding the right plants is especially important in a windowsill garden, where space and growing environment are fixed.

When designing a windowsill garden, you will want to determine the best shape and size for the plants you choose. Windowsills can offer large areas for displaying plants, or they can be small and cramped. When you buy a plant, you might select it in an early growth period, when it is not clear what the mature plant will look like. It is important to understand how large your plant will grow and what its general shape and growth habit will be.

The following guide will help you understand the types of leaves, stems, and other characteristics that can give you clues to a plant's identity and needs. Plants come in five main categories, and within each category are sub-categories based on factors like the shape of the leaves, the presence or absence of spines, fragrance, and size. At the highest level, all plants will fall into one of the following categories:

- Plants with small oranges present
- Plants with no ordinary leaves
- Plants with spines or hairs on leaves or stems
- Plants with no spines but with flower
- Plants with no spines and no flowers

In addition to the above characteristics of houseplants, each plant will also have a specific size, shape, and growth pattern. All plants grow in characteristic patterns called growth habits. Houseplant habits are canopy-like (large palms), cascading (wandering Jews), fountain-shaped (caladiums), rosette-shaped (hen and chicks), shrub-like (umbrella plant), or tree-like (ficus).

Plants that remain small may grow to be no more than 18 inches, which is ideal for a small area. Medium-sized plants may grow 18 to 36 inches, and large plants may reach 6 to 10 feet. In some cases, you can control the growth and size of plants. Obviously, you are unlikely to control a large plant such as a date palm, but many plants can respond to special growth care.

By keeping plants in small pots, you limit the extent to which the roots will grow; however, be prepared for some leaf dieback as the roots become unable to support all the foliage. You can also clip back leaves, trim the tops of plants, or prune the roots to keep the plant at a certain size. Bonsai plants are an excellent example of these principles. While bonsai plants are normally small, slow-growing plants by nature, gardeners limit their growth through selective trimming and root control.

However, if you are unwilling or unable to devote the extra time and care that it takes to keep a plant small, make sure you choose a species that will maintain the size and shape you desire without additional work.

Keeping Pets and Children Safe from Toxic Houseplants

Some of the strongest poisons in the world are produced by plants. Many houseplants are naturally equipped with toxic chemicals to ward off the wandering leaf-eaters. In nature, this is a good protective mechanism for a plant's survival. Although bringing these plants into homes has decreased the risk of the leaf-eating predator, the naturally occurring chemical toxins have not decreased.

Many people are not aware that there are houseplants that can be toxic to humans and animals. Some plants can cause skin irritation or rashes if touched, while others can be harmful or fatal if swallowed. Toxic plants range from life-threatening to merely irritating, but a plant that can be irritating to the skin of an adult could cause a fatal rash to a small child or animal. In addition, small children and animals do not understand that the spines and hairs of cacti and the thorns of plants can hurt them. Make sure you place these out of reach as well.

The following list of toxic houseplants is not exhaustive, but covers many of the most common plants you will find in stores and from suppliers. Listed below is the common name for each plant, its Latin name, and possible symptoms from touching or ingesting certain parts of the plant:

- Aloe vera (*Aloe barbadensis*): Some people will experience irritation of the intestinal tract, vomiting, and diarrhea if they swallow aloe vera juice. However, many people drink aloe vera juice for health with no side effects.

- Amaryllis (*Amaryllis*): Toxic to cats and dogs. If ingested, it may cause vomiting, depression, diarrhea, abdominal pain, hypersalivation, anorexia, or tremors.

- Arrowhead plant (*Syngonium podophyllum*): This plant is toxic when ingested, causing the throat, lips, and mouth to burn. It may also cause vomiting.

- Asparagus fern (*Asparagus densiflorus*): The berries and sap on the asparagus fern are considered toxic. Eating the berries can cause gastrointestinal problems. Coming into contact with the sap may cause skin irritation, swelling, and blisters.

- Azalea (*Rhododendron occidentale*): All parts of this plant are toxic if ingested. Symptoms may include depression, nausea, vomiting, diarrhea, abdominal pain, watery eyes and nose, and loss of energy.

- Bird-of-Paradise (*Poinciana gilliesii*): The toxic parts of this plant are the raw seeds. If ingested, they may cause nausea, diarrhea, and vomiting.

- Caladium (*Caladium spp.*): All parts of this plant are toxic if ingested. Look for symptoms such as burning and swelling of the tongue, lips, and mouth; nausea; vomiting; and diarrhea. Contact with sap may also cause skin irritation.

- Christmas rose (*Helleborus niger L.*): All parts of this plant are toxic but only if large quantities are ingested. Symptoms may include burning and swelling of the tongue, lips, and mouth; nausea; abdominal cramping; depression; and diarrhea. Contact with sap may cause minor skin irritation.

- Chrysanthemum (*Chrysanthemum X morifolium*): Extended exposure to garden mums can cause contact dermatitis, with symptoms being redness, scaling, and blistering.

- Creeping fig (*Ficus spp.*): Coming into contact with the sap of the creeping fig can cause itchy eyes, coughing, and wheezing.

- Croton (*Codiaeum variegatum*): The bark of this plant can cause mouth and throat irritation if ingested.

- Crown of thorns (*Euphorbia milii*): The sap of this plant is the most toxic. Ingesting the sap can cause vomiting, nausea, or diarrhea. Handling some species of this plant can cause skin irritations, eye irritation, and blistering.

- Dumbcane (*Dieffenbachia spp.*): This plant causes mouth irritation, numbness, and swelling.

- English ivy (*Hedera helix*): This plant can cause many reactions, from a blistering skin rash from contact with the sap to vomiting and difficulty breathing if eaten.

- Holly (*Ilex spp.*): The fruit of the holly plant is very toxic for children and animals. Ingesting the berries can causes vomiting, blurred vision, convulsions, difficulty breathing, or irregular heartbeat.

- Iris (*Iris spp.*): The bulbs of the iris plant are considered toxic and can cause gastrointestinal symptoms.

- Jerusalem cherry (*Solanum pseudocapsicum*): The entire Jerusalem cherry plant is toxic, especially the berries. If ingested, it may cause scratchy throat, diarrhea, fever, and gastric irritation.

- Lily-of-the-Valley (*Convallaria majalis*): Although this plant is not toxic to the touch, it can have severe symptoms if ingested. Possible symptoms include vomiting, diarrhea, dizziness, confusion, and headaches.

- Mistletoe (*Phoradendron flavescens*): Poisoning from mistletoe is rare, but it can create toxic symptoms such as vomiting, urinating more than normal, diarrhea, or hypersalivation in pets if they ingest large quantities of the berries.

- Philodendron leaves (*Philodendron spp.*): These leaves can produce an itchy skin rash if eaten.

- Poinsettia (*Euphorbia pulcherrima*): Swallowing any part of this plant can cause mouth irritation, vomiting, and nausea.

- All pothos varieties (*Epipremnum aureum*): These plants will cause vomiting if eaten.

- Sago palm (*Cycas revoluta*): The fleshy leaves and seeds of the sago palm will cause vomiting, headaches, diarrhea, and dizziness if ingested.

- Umbrella plant (*Schefflera actinophylla*): Ingesting the leaves of the umbrella plant can cause vomiting, numbness and tingling of the mouth, and lack of coordination. Coming into contact with the sap can cause skin irritation.

- Swiss cheese plant/Split-leaf philodendron (*Monstera deliciosa*): Eating the leaves of this plant can cause your mouth and throat to burn.

- Wax begonia (*Begonia semperflorens-cultorum*): The roots, tubers, and rhizomes of the wax begonia are toxic if ingested. Look for symptoms such as burning of mouth, throat, lips, and tongue; swelling; difficulty with speech and swallowing; and possibly nausea and vomiting.

If you suspect a pet or a child has eaten any part of a toxic plant or has been exposed to a poisonous one, call poison control immediately and provide aid as they direct you. Contact the American Association of Poison Control Centers online at **www.aapcc.org/DNN** or by phone 1-800-222-1222 for more information.

Start with Seeds or Start with Plants?

Every gardener has his or her own preferences about how to start a new plant — with either a seedling or a handful of seeds. In some cases, the decision may amount only to personal preference. In others, it may come down to the time of year, the cost of the plants and seeds, and the ease of growing a plant from a seed.

It is important to note: Not all plants are easily grown from seed and are instead divided or planted from cuttings to create new plants. Local nurseries will have ample information about plants best grown from cuttings.

Why start with seeds?

Seeds are invariably cheaper than buying seedlings. For the same price as a few young plants, a gardener can buy enough seeds to grow a field of plants. The price alone tempts many indoor gardeners into trying to grow many plants from seeds. Because a packet of seeds is inexpensive, gardeners can attempt to grow many plants at once.

Choosing to grow with seeds is also a way to continue growing the same plants that you have grown and enjoyed before. Saving the seeds from your herbs and flowers will allow you to grow the progeny, or offspring, of the plant that you enjoyed.

If you have very little space and want to grow plants indoors in containers, growing seeds is a good way to grow a large number of plants without taking up a lot of room. Seed trays may house 50 or more seedlings in just the space of a small tabletop. Your windowsill garden could incorporate seedlings you intend to grow indoors through the life of the plant or seedlings you intend to plant outdoors once reaching a certain size.

Why start with plants?

Some plants simply do not grow well from seeds. Others may be propagated from seeds, but the process of getting the seeds to germinate and the seedling to grow into a smaller plant is extremely complicated and can take months. For example, mint and basil are both herbal plants that are great for use in windowsill gardens. Basil is easily grown from seed, while it is not recommended that a beginner grow mint from a seed.

Another advantage to starting a windowsill garden with plants instead of seeds is the instant gratification factor. Growing from seeds can be a lengthy, boring task. If you are teaching children how to garden, they may lose interest long before the seeds germinate. With plants, you get to see the plants from day one instead of waiting weeks or even months.

Finding Seeds

Starting a plant or herb windowsill garden from seeds can be difficult and time-consuming. However, there are several distinct advantages to using them. Among those is the readiness of finding even the most exotic seeds.

When you begin to look for seeds sold at stores, you will begin to notice how pervasive they are. They are sold in most mass-merchandise, hardware, home improvement, and gardening stores. In addition, there are also many seed catalogs available to order seeds by mail. Online seed stores may specialize in certain types of seeds, such as roses or exotic plants, while others sell hundreds of different plant seeds.

Unless you buy very exotic, rare seeds, most seed packets are extremely inexpensive. Less than $5 can generally purchase several seed packets, even if the seeds are bought online or through a catalog and must be shipped to you. *See Chapter 9 for instructions on propagating through seeds.*

Finding Healthy and Affordable Plants

There are numerous markets for finding houseplants, including florists, greenhouses, home improvement and hardware stores, nurseries, craft fairs, mail-order catalogs, farmers markets, and even by taking cuttings from the plants of friends and family. Acquiring plants from these different outlets will offer varying quality and health guarantees, which are important factors when buying new plants.

Buying your plants from a florist *may* mean that you will be able to take advantage of a plant expert's knowledge, but remember, a florist's main business is caring for cut flowers, and live plants may just be a side interest. Going to a top-end supplier, such as a plant nursery, may provide the most assistance. Just be sure to seek help from a houseplant expert. Home improvement or department stores can be great sources for the same plants found at high-end nurseries, but at a lower price. The main difference between the two sources will be the health of the plant.

Houseplants can be found just about everywhere you shop. Common sources for finding healthy and affordable specimens for your windowsill garden might include any combination of the following:

- Local nurseries
- Garden centers

- Garden shows
- Florists
- Farmers markets
- University horticulture departments
- Mail-order/online catalogs
- Supermarkets
- Mega-stores
- Home improvement centers
- Hardware stores

Whichever market you choose, first impressions are important. Look across all the plants you can see, not just the variety you want to purchase. As you peruse the plants, ask yourself these questions to evaluate the available selection of plants:

- Do the plants look unhealthy or sickly?
- Do you see signs of pest infestations or rampant disease?
- Do the blooms look brilliant or faded?
- Are there signs of new growth?
- Do the leaves look perky or droopy?

Answering these questions as you are scanning the plants will help you determine whether to stay and dig deeper into the selection or move on to the next shop on your list.

Best selection and most reliable

Local nurseries, garden centers, and garden shows are by far the best places to shop for and purchase houseplants. These suppliers specialize in all kinds of plants. They can probably even help you organize your windowsill garden from scratch. There are experts available to tell you all about the plants you seek. These suppliers often provide a better selection and healthier plants. Another benefit to shopping at one of these locations is that they hold regular seminars or workshops for a specific category of plants, such as houseplants, perennials, or herb gardens.

- **Make your own personal list** — Bring a list with you of the plants you have researched that will be ideal for your windowsill garden. Be as specific as possible with the common name and Latin name of the plant you have on your list. This will help the nursery staff quickly locate the plant species you have requested.

- **Gather reference material** — Before making your purchases, procure a catalog or list of the plants in stock at the local nursery, garden center, or garden show booth. Use your own personal list and the nursery's plant list to make comparisons and to take notes as you wander through the aisles or visit the vendor tables at the garden show.

Nurseries, garden centers, and garden shows provide you with two important things for buying and selecting plants for your windowsill garden: selection and reliability. You will have to do a little bit more legwork to get the quality and price you want for your plants.

Premium and specialty plants

Florists, farmers markets, and university horticulture department are known for selling premium plants or preparing plants for a certain holiday (such as Christmas or Easter) or special event (such as weddings). Although plants from these sources tend to be higher priced, they are also high in quality.

Florists — If you intend to work directly with a florist, keep in mind the functions of the two different types of florists:

- *Wholesale florist*: A wholesale florist will supply the retailer with fresh-cut flowers and potted plants. They might sell directly to flower shops, or they may sell through wholesale produce and farmers markets. Keep in mind that some wholesale florists are growers as well, so you may be able to get premium plants through this source.

- *Retail florist*: Retail florists range in size and function, from kiosks in shopping malls and hospital gift shops to larger, independent flower shops. Retail florists specialize in providing arrangements for special occasions and events. If they do not have a specific houseplant in stock, they often know a supplier and can order you exactly what you want. Remember, it will cost more because a retail florist does not specialize in houseplants.

Farmers markets — Part of the seasonal summer and autumn routine involves attending a weekend farmers market where you can find some rare and special plants. These plants have usually been home-grown under the care of a knowledgeable person. However, reliable information on water, light, soil requirements, and general plant care usually does not come with these plants.

Herbs are a common find at farmers markets. They are often in good health because they have not had to endure the trauma of transportation from another climate.

Universities — University horticulture departments can be a unique place to find rare and crossbred plant species. The quality of the plants from universities is optimal because they have access to the proper environments for growing their plants. The assortment of plants can be limiting because these are not nurseries for the general public. If you live in a town or city that is near a university, contact the horticulture department to see if they have any specials on seasonal plants. Many horticulture departments will sell poinsettias during Christmas or lilies during Easter to generate income for their department.

The main point to remember about buying and selecting plants from a florist, farmers market, or a university horticulture department is that they will be high-quality plants, but may also be on the pricier side.

Vast selection online, but proceed with caution

If you deal with a mail-order or online plant company, you rely solely on the company's reputation and money-back guarantee. If you are planting a garden from seed, you may have less recourse — but you may also have put less investment into your plants. Many reputable companies provide high-quality plants.

Buying plants through catalogs gives you access to a wide variety of plants, including rare and possibly expensive specimens. Mail orders can often be cheaper than the local market. However, you take more risks when ordering by mail.

Before buying plant from any online or mail-order nursery, do some homework first. Check out the Better Business Bureau's website (**www.bbb.org**) for information on the supplier, including the number of complaints they have received in the last 12 to 48 months, and whether those complaints were resolved satisfactorily.

Do not do business with companies showing an unsatisfactory rating. The Garden Watchdog website (**davesgarden.com/products/gwd**) is an online resource that reviews mail-order and online nurseries. Their site provides a large collection of user reviews for hundreds of nurseries.

Although mail-order and online catalogs provide some of the largest selection of plants, consider the following helpful hints before adding anything to your shopping cart:

- **Understand the payment terms**. A mail-order nursery's payment policies will tell you much about the business. Never pay through cash or money orders only; these methods are unsecure and untraceable. It may be impossible to get a refund if the sale is unsatisfactory.

- **Research the seller's facilities**. Does the nursery have an actual retail building? While nurseries with only an online storefront can be perfectly reputable, it can be helpful to work with a physical location. Often a nursery that grows its own plants, rather than a mail-order or online distributor, will take more pride and care with the products. In addition, a retail "brick-and-mortar" business can be more reliable.

- **Understand ordering policies**. Many mail-order companies will substitute a similar item when your selection is sold out. Order forms often have a box to check to indicate that you do not want substitutions. If there is not a box to check on the order form, clearly state that you do not want them to make any substitutions. Reputable sellers either will refrain from shipping during periods of extreme cold or will put protective wrap in the box to keep plants from freezing. Make sure your dealer will make every effort to send plants safely to you.

- **Clarify refund and replacement policy.** Many mail-order companies have a refund or replacement policy for defective plants. The company usually gives you enough time to plant the item and inspect its growth. Be sure you understand the cut-off date by which the business must be notified of problems or plant failures, and communicate with them before the cut-off date.

- **Keep a record of your purchases.** Online companies often send an online invoice or confirmation e-mail when you place an order. Keep this information and record names, item numbers, prices, and dates of your purchases to facilitate any communications between you and the company.

- **Check your plants carefully.** When you receive a houseplant or bulb from a mail-order company, check the package carefully. Make sure there is no damage to the outside of the package. Then open the package and inspect the inner wrap for damage, bugs, or fungus. If anything is wrapped in plastic, open it to allow proper circulation. Check the box for any instructions on temporary handling or special planting instructions. It may be helpful to mist the products, as shipping can be a lengthy, dry process.

- **Secure credit card payment.** Paying by credit card or through online services such as PayPal™ (**www.paypal.com**) will offer you — and the seller — protection and a secure payment method. PayPal is a merchant service that allows its members to accept credit card payments online.

Although the option of purchasing online still holds a higher risk than shopping at your local nursery or garden center, it can be a viable resource for you after you have taken the necessary precautions. Once you have conducted the necessary research and made it through your first purchase successfully, your world to healthy and affordable houseplants will be opened further. Online plant retailers tend to have a greater variety of plants than your local nursery, so they can offer a larger selection.

Large assortment at lower prices

Supermarkets, mega-stores, home improvement centers, and hardware stores can offer one of the largest assortments of foliage and flowering plants at a fairly low price. These suppliers often receive new plants twice a week so you can enjoy some good buys on healthy plants. If you know when a shipment will be coming in, try to shop right after the shipment has been stocked. This will prevent your plants from sitting for a long time, and plant care and quality can vary from supplier to supplier. Resist the urge to buy low-quality plants at a bargain price. Use the following tips to select the best plants from these suppliers:

- Inspect the plant carefully. You want a plant with perky, bright, green foliage. Stems should not be limp but solid and firm. The plant should look fresh, not off-colored or bruised. Check the soil to ensure that it is not fluffy, which is an indication that a soilless mix was used. The pot should feel on the heavier side when you lift it.

- Check the plant for insects and disease. Start by examining the top and undersides of the leaves. Brown or white streaks on the leaves can be an indication of rot or disease. Leaves that have chewed edges are a sign that insects have been or are currently present in the soil. Give the plant a gentle shake; if whiteflies are present, they will hover around the plant like a cloud.

- Perform a quick soil check. Avoid buying plants that are growing in dry, caked soil. This is an indication that the plant has been stressed by drought.

If you know what you are looking for and select carefully, you can acquire healthy and affordable plants from supermarkets, mega-stores, home improvement centers, or hardware stores. One of the best things to know about these sources is the day they receive their plant stock. Ask the manager when the store receives its weekly plant stock, and be sure to visit on those days. You will quickly be able to tell the new plants from the ones that have been sitting on the shelves for a while.

Knowing how to read the signs

The key to selecting healthy, long-living plants is in knowing how to read the signs. Before you go shopping, first learn more about the kind of plants that would be best for your home environment. Knowing the general characteristics and specific needs of the plants will allow you to make better decisions and buy the right plant for the right environment. *Chapters 2 through 5 provide comprehensive profiles for foliage plants, fragrant plants, flowering plants, and herbal plants.* You will have access to information about each plant with respect to temperature and humidity, light requirement, soil type and fertilizing, care and propagation, and common pests and diseases. Having this information readily available allows you to determine which plants will be most suitable for your windowsill garden.

Seed of Knowledge: When you are shopping, be sure the label matches the common and scientific name of the plant you want.

There are four primary areas to evaluate on a plant indicating whether or not it will survive.

Leave it up to the leaves — Begin by evaluating the leaves. They should be the proper color, shape, and size for that plant species. The leaves should not have dry, brown edges, blemishes, or discolored areas. They should not look wilted or droopy, and the leaves toward the bottom of the stem should not be pale or yellow. If the plant looks like it has been recently pruned, or there is evidence of over-pruning, this might indicate that the plant had a disease. Do not be afraid to ask questions about the status of the plant you are considering.

The shape of things to come — Next, check the shape of the plant. While each plant species has a characteristic shape, the plant you are considering should not look long and leggy with sparse leaves. It should not have a heavy bunch of leaves at the top with misshapen or sparse under-foliage. Climbing or vining plants should have several vines, not one long stem with leaves scattered along the length. As a general rule of thumb, purchase vining plants that look bushy, because over time the vines will develop into a lovely cascade. The leaves and stems should be free of insects, disease, scarring, blemishes, or broken twigs. *See Chapter 10 for pest and disease identification.*

Bring the soil to the surface — The soil gives further clues to the plant's health. In lower-quality markets, the soil is likely to be thin, loose, and peaty. The pots may be too small for the plants so the roots cover the surface and grow from the holes at the bottom of the pot. Mass-grown plants are usually nurtured in cheap plastic pots and overexposed to artificial light to speed growth. While this is not a particular concern as you purchase a plant, assume they will need immediate repotting and some special attention while they become acclimated to a new environment. If the plant's pot is full of soil and you do not see any roots, then it has probably just been transplanted. The healthiest plants have an equal soil-to-root ratio.

When everything is in bloom — If you are shopping for a flowering plant, choose one where most of the flower buds are still tight or just ready to bloom. It may be fun to bring home a plant in full bloom, but if it does not bloom again for several months, you will not get the full pleasure of a "showy" plant. If there are no blooms on the plant, make sure you know exactly the color and shape of the flowers.

Do not be afraid to ask questions about a plant before buying it. Find out how much fertilizer, light, and humidity it needs, as well as when you should repot it. Once you have found the healthy plants you want, pick several of the healthiest plants and set them to the side. Look them over once more for the signs mentioned above, and be sure none have any un-noticed problems. Then, through process of elimination, select the plants you want to buy.

Required Tools for Plant Care

It is important to gather the right tools before you start your windowsill garden. This will ensure that a gardening emergency can be solved before it gets out of control. These basic tools can be used for a wide variety of plants. These tools will be especially handy for scenarios that require you to transport a plant to another container or outdoors, when you are initially planting your foliage, or when maintaining the design of your windowsill garden.

To save time and money when gardening, invest in a good, sturdy set of gardening tools and accessories. Though they will be more expensive up front, there will be no need to replace worn-out or bent tools that do not hold up over time. You will not be stuck with broken tools as your plants outgrow their pots. High-quality gardening tools can be found in big-box home improvement stores, gardening catalogs, and online gardening stores.

Gloves

Gloves may not be necessary in all cases. If you only want to grow a few small plants with smooth leaves and no thorns, you may not need them at all. However, if you plan to do a good deal of gardening, using gloves can keep

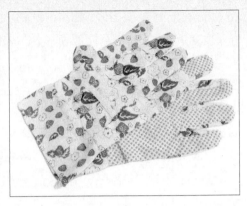

your skin from becoming rougher due to the constant contact with the soil and the plants. It is always better to wear gloves when gardening, if only to prevent incidents like infected cuts or rashes. While not always best for outdoor use, cloth gloves work well when working on your windowsill garden. They are inexpensive, comfortable, and will provide protection without encumbering your movements.

Trowel

A trowel is a tool that can be used for many different gardening tasks. This long, slender hand shovel can be used to mix your potting soil and fertilizer before your plant is planted. It can also be used to dig seed holes in the

soil. Narrower trowels are useful for separating seedlings and digging out dead plants from among living ones. A wider trowel can be used like any other hand shovel, transplanting growing plants and digging out weeds that need to be removed. Choose a thicker trowel to avoid bending it and rendering it useless. A trowel with thicker metal will be more expensive, but it will save time and hassle in the end.

Clippers

Anyone who grows windowsill plants will need clippers of various sizes. A small set of clippers can be used to cut away dead flowers and leaves cleanly. If you want to prune a plant that has thick stems, a pair of clippers or pruning shears is es-

sential for making it through the stem in one cut to avoid damaging the stem. With shears that are too small or too dull, you may strip or crush the stem instead of making a clean cut.

Watering can

While a watering can is not nec-essarily essential, it is a conve-nient tool to have. If your plants are small, you might be able to water your plants with a drinking glass; however, refilling it many times to water all of the plants

will add to the time it takes to care for your windowsill garden. A water-ing can may be used for inside and can be filled quickly. One watering can should be useful for all indoor tasks.

Watering cans come in metal, plastic, and ceramic. Ceramic can crack, chip, and break — not the features you want in a tool that will get plenty of use. Metal watering cans are made to be functional, beautiful, and du-rable. Brass and copper are used in some of the higher-end watering cans. Plastic watering cans range from very inexpensive, simply designed models to higher-end versions that have long spouts and some metal parts. Some of the most expensive plastic watering cans have plastic bodies and handles and metal spouts. It would be best to get a long spout to be sure you reach the soil of your windowsill plant.

Cultivating fork

A cultivating fork looks like a trowel, but the end has pointed tines — the pointed ends of the tool — instead of a rounded edge. Some cultivating forks have tines that are straight, while others have bent tines to allow the tool to provide more leverage. The bent designs resemble hoes that have a few tines on one end instead of a solid, flat end.

This tool can be useful for tilling small areas of soil or creating a depression in which to place seeds. A cultivating fork might not be of much help with planting in potting soil or for taking plants out of a container to repot them, but it can be helpful if you have to repot any of your plants.

String or garden ties

Some plants need to have firm support while growing. This is especially important when the plant is being grown in a container inside and cannot trail away to the nearest fence or tree.

Vines often need to be tied in order for them to grow in small spaces. Some gardeners use ordinary household string, pipe cleaners, twist ties, or yarn to hold plants in place. These have to be checked periodically and retied as the plant grows to allow the plant to do so without being pulled downward by the ties. There are also plant ties that are specially made to stretch with the plant as it grows so that it does not have to be changed as often.

Stakes

Stakes are needed for some smaller plants that cannot support themselves. If you want to grow orchids, stakes are necessary for holding up the long, narrow stems. Orchid growers can tie their orchid to a stake, but many prefer to use colorful plant clips to gently keep the stem in place against the stake. Stakes can help to create a smaller area for the plant without stifling its growth.

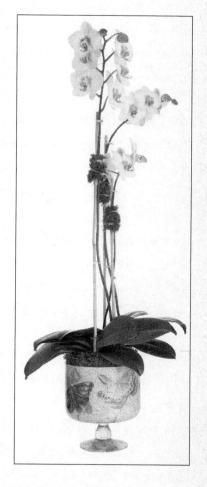

If you supply a stake or trellis for a plant, you should plant the seeds or seedling directly at the base of the support. This will enable the plant to grow directly upward onto the support without much early vine training to get the plant to climb the support. With a support directly above the plant, a plant with vines will begin climbing as soon as it is tall enough to do so.

If you need a stake for a flowering plant, use the shortest one possible. The stake should be slightly shorter than the full height of the mature plant. This will ensure that the stake will not be readily seen when looking at the flowers.

Making Your New Plants Feel at Home

A degree of care is necessary when you bring new plants home from a store. Some plants have trouble when moved, and many tropical plants will suffer from extreme changes in climate. Once the plant is home, you will want to take a few precautions to make sure the plant adjusts well to its new environment.

First, you must protect plants from cold or hot weather during transport. Even a slight drop in temperature can shock a plant. If you move a plant in cold weather, start your car and turn on the heat before bringing the plant out. Wrap your new plant in a plastic bag, such as a dry cleaner's or shopping bag, before leaving the nursery. In extremely warm weather, shelter the plant from the sun with an opaque bag, and make sure the car is cool before putting the plant inside. Never leave a plant in a car during hot or cold weather — even a few minutes in a severe temperature can permanently damage your purchase.

Once you get your plant home, keep it in a separate room away from other plants for at least two weeks. During this time, any problems such as insect infestation, disease, or mistreatment will appear. You can return such plants for a refund or replacement. Mist the plant daily and provide adequate water. During this time, you can also determine if the plant's pot and soil are optimal for its health.

When you get the plant home, it is a good idea to clean it to remove any dust, contaminants, or lingering pests that could infect your house. A solution of ½ teaspoon of dish soap and ½ teaspoon of vinegar in 12 ounces of warm water will make a gentle cleaner and pesticide. Wipe the foliage and stems with a cloth dampened in the solution.

The following chapters will introduce you to a wide variety of plants and their specific needs. Chapter 9 explains the various propagation methods, while Chapter 10 discusses the pests and diseases you may come across and how to remedy these problems.

Chapter 2

Add Texture to Your Home with Foliage Plants

Most houseplants can be grouped into two broad categories — those known for their foliage, and those known for their flowers. This chapter will focus on a variety of plants that have interesting textures, shapes, variegations, and sizes. Chapter 3 will discuss more than a dozen plant species that are known for their "showy" blooms, and Chapter 4 will introduce you to a variety of herbal plants you can use for cooking and medicinal purposes. For each plant profiled in this chapter, you will discover its common and botanical names; a brief description of the plant; temperature and humidity preferences; light, watering, soil, and fertilizing requirements; techniques for care and propagation; pests and diseases that are common to the plant; and interesting facts you may not have known about each plant.

Aloe vera

Common name(s): Aloe vera, healing aloe, medicine plant, burn plant

Botanical name: *Aloe barbadensis*

Plant description: Aloe vera is a succulent that is native to sunny, dry locations such as deserts. It grows long, fleshy spikes that are

medium green and usually spotted with lighter green. The edges of the spiky leaves are lined with thorns.

Light requirements: Aloe vera needs bright light, preferably from an east or south window. However, aloe plants grown indoors should be introduced to direct sunlight gradually so the spikes do not burn. Burned spikes will appear reddish, but if not too badly damaged, they will return to their normal green color. Aloe will also grow in medium- and low-light conditions.

Temperature and humidity: Aloe likes average room temperatures between 65 to 75 degrees. The plant can be grown outdoors during summer months if it is introduced to sunlight slowly and does not receive too much water. Bring the plant indoors before the first frost.

Watering: Like most succulents, aloe vera will rot if watered too frequently, so allow the soil to dry out completely before watering again, and then water sparingly. Rinse the leaves once a year in a gentle, lukewarm shower to rid them of dust and debris.

Soil and fertilizing: Aloe has short root systems and grows best in a sand mixture of two parts sand to one part gardening soil. Fertilize once or twice a year with a diluted general-purpose fertilizer.

Care and propagation: Propagate aloe vera from offsets in spring or early summer. You can also carefully divide the rootstock.

Common pests and diseases: Mealybugs are suspect because they can hide in the rosette folds.

Other points of interest: This plant is one of the easiest species for beginning gardeners to grow. The juices of aloe help heal burns and are often used in cosmetics and skin products.

Aluminum plant

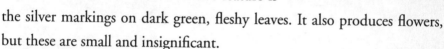

Common name(s): Aluminum plant, watermelon pilea

Botanical name: *Pilea cadierei*

Plant description: A Vietnamese native, the aluminum plant is a bushy plant with somewhat oval leaves. Its most attractive feature is the silver markings on dark green, fleshy leaves. It also produces flowers, but these are small and insignificant.

Light requirements: This plant requires moderate to bright light from an east or west window.

Temperature and humidity: The aluminum plant prefers 45 percent shade and average temperatures of 60 to 70 degrees. This plant likes moderate to high humidity.

Watering: Keep the soil slightly moist without allowing the roots to stand in water.

Soil and fertilizing: These plants grow best in a sandy, well-drained soil a blend of two parts sand, one part planting soil, and one part peat moss. The plant requires evenly moist soil; the leaf edges will begin to turn brown and dry if the soil dries out completely.

Care and propagation: The older the plant, the more it tends to drop the lower leaves, and the stems can become hard and woody. Pinch off new growth to keep the plant bushy. If the plant is old, take a cutting from young growth and discard the old plant.

Common pests and diseases: Watch for mealybugs and spider mites as potential pests for this plant.

Other points of interest: Aluminum plants are most attractive when they are young and bushy. Keep them bushy by pinching terminal buds. Parts of this plant are poisonous if ingested.

Artillery plant

Common name(s): Artillery plant, gunpowder plant

Botanical name: *Pilea trianthemoides*

Plant description: The artillery plant is a creeping plant with dense, fern-like foliage on arching stems. It is a native of tropical, humid areas such as Florida and Hawaii. The tiny leaves are usually a medium green or lime color, but one cultivar produces leaves with variegated pink foliage.

Photo By Forest and Kim Starr

The name "artillery plant" comes from the plant's habit of shooting pollen during the flowering season.

Light requirements: Artillery plants enjoy low to medium light; exposure to direct sunlight will cause the leaves to turn brown and fall off.

Temperature and humidity: This plant thrives in average to high temperatures and humidity levels. Be sure to avoid cold drafts.

Watering: Water regularly, but do not overwater.

Soil and fertilizing: Pot the plant in an all-purpose potting mix and allow the soil to dry out before watering. Make sure the pot has good drainage to prevent root rot. Fertilize the plant every other month with a half-strength solution of a balanced fertilizer.

Care and propagation: This plant also thrives with occasional leaf misting. To propagate the artillery plant, divide the root ball or take stem cuttings.

Common pests and diseases: On occasion, artillery plants are pestered by chewing insects. Also watch for root rot in poorly drained soils.

Other points of interest: Artillery plants are known as "hard-to-kill" plants. Although they will not live forever, these plants can grow for a year or more even in the poorest conditions. Artillery plants can quickly become weeds because seeds germinate quickly in the soil.

Baby's tears

Common name(s): Baby's tears, Irish moss, Corsican mint, angel tears, peace in the home, helxine, mother of thousands

Botanical name: *Soleirolia soleirolii*

Plant description: This is a small, creeping plant with masses of small, round leaves on thin stems. As the plant grows, its bright green leaves will cascade over the side of a pot and drape down a windowsill. The plant is a native of Corsica, where it grows wild in shady, moist areas.

Light requirements: Baby's tears grow well in semi-sunny or shady locations.

Temperature and humidity: It thrives in high humidity but is not a good candidate for a terrarium because it needs good air circulation. It grows best in cooler temperatures, from 60 to 75 degrees.

Watering: Keep evenly moist at all times. Do not let dry out. This plant can stand in water without damage to the roots.

Soil and fertilizing: The plant appreciates rich, well-drained soil that remains constantly moist but not waterlogged. Fertilize this plant every two weeks with a diluted all-purpose fertilizer.

Care and propagation: The leaves will grow well if rinsed once or twice a year in a gentle, lukewarm shower. The plants propagate easily by simply pressing part of the stem into the soil, where it will soon take root. The rooted plantlet can then be cut from the main plant right next to the rooted section. Alternatively, you can start new plants from stem tip cuttings.

Common pests and diseases: Dry soil and excessive minerals can cause root damage, and aphids are suspect as a pests for this plant.

Other points of interest: Trimming the baby's tears plant will cause it to grow into a little mound, like a moss. Because of its small size, it is a perfect plant for a windowsill with little room. It is especially attractive when placed as a contrast next to plants with long, textured, or vertically growing foliage.

Burro's tail

Common name(s): Burro's tail, donkey's tail, lamb's tail

Botanical name: *Sedum morganianum*

Plant description: Burro's tail is an interesting succulent native to Mexico and Honduras. It is a hanging plant that grows long columns of fleshy stems with small overlapping leaves. The leaves are a blue-green color and are shaped like grains of wheat. The shape is that of an animal's tail, which gives the plant its name. When grown in the wild, the plant will produce clustered, pink flowers, but these rarely appear in cultivated plants.

Light requirements: Place it in a windowsill that receives full sun and it will thrive.

Temperature and humidity: Suitable temperatures for this plant in the spring, summer, and fall range from 68 to 90 degrees. In the winter, this plant prefers an average temperature of 65 degrees.

Watering: Allow the soil to become dry to the touch before watering.

Soil and fertilizing: Plant in a sandy cactus mix. Fertilize once or twice a year with a diluted general-purpose fertilizer, being careful not to get any on the foliage.

Care and propagation: This plant can be propagated through stem cuttings or leaf cuttings, rooting after a few days.

Common pests and diseases: Be careful not to overwater this plant because its small delicate roots are prone to root rot. Mealybugs, slugs, snails, and scale insects are all possible problems for the burro's tail plant.

Other points of interest: Burro's tail is one of the easiest to care for plants because it wants to be left alone. When moved or touched, it tends to shed its fleshy leaves. Burro's tail is ideal for rock gardens and as hanging plants.

Cacti

Plant description: The cacti family of plants is a subspecies of succulents. Their unusual shapes and amazing variety provide fun opportunities for windowsill arrangements. Cacti are plants that grow wild in desert regions of the Americas. Generally, cacti are fleshy plants that store water; most have spines or hairs that protect them from predators and the sun, and most have shallow roots systems designed to catch maximum water in brief desert rainstorms. Several varieties of cactus plants produce showy flowers in interesting shapes and textures. Most cacti grow relatively slowly, but several types can grow from 4 to 20 feet tall over time. Purchase the size that will fit on your windowsill and you can be assured that the plant will fit your space for a great deal of time; cacti can be long-living specimens. There are several types of cacti that are most commonly grown as houseplants, such as:

- **Ball cactus** (*Epithelantha spp.*) — The ball cactus is round with symmetrical thorny ridges growing from the cap to the root ball.

- **Pincushion cactus** (*Pediocactus spp.*) — Pincushion cacti are globe-shaped with whorls of rice-shaped leaves spiraling down from the top of the plant.

- **Bunny ears cactus** (*Opuntia microdasys*) — Bunny ears cactus has paddle-shaped leaves that grow one upon the other in vertical lines from a central plant; this variety is dotted with clusters of thorns.

- **Bishop's cap cactus** (*Astrophytum myriostigma*) — Bishop's cap is an exceptionally exotic-looking gray-green specimen with three to eight ribs, but usually five. Its sweet-smelling yellow flowers bloom during the summer and are usually followed by a reddish fruit. This cactus has no spines.

- **Old man cactus** (*Cephalocereus senilis*) — Old man cacti form a medium green column that is covered with wispy white hairs; hooked spines are located under the hairs.

- **Star cactus** (*Astrophytum asterias*) — The star cactus, in a shape indicative of its name, forms groups of small oval stems that are covered with sharp, interwoven spines.

- **Golden barrel cactus** (*Echinocactus grusonii*) — Golden barrel is another spherical cactus that has golden spines running down its ridges; at the top of the plant, the spines are softer and form a golden cap.

Light requirements: Most cacti need bright sunlight. Even full sun is usually not a problem for these staunch plants.

Temperature and humidity: Cacti are generally heat-resistant and often not bothered by rising spring temperatures or intense summer heat. In the fall and winter, however, most cacti prefer a cool place to rest in a minimally heated room that is allowed to cool to 60 degrees at night.

Watering: Let the soil dry out completely before watering again. Water only the surface of the soil when needed, about once a month. Cacti are easily killed by over-watering. If you see the plant turning yellow and squishy, especially at the base of the plant, it is a sign that over-watering has caused the plant to rot. When a cactus is receiving too little water, it will usually turn a darker color and appear to shrink in on itself. It will quickly recover unless it is so damaged that it begins to brown.

Soil and fertilizing: Plant cacti in a sandy cactus blend, making sure to protect your hands from spines by wrapping the plant in cloth or paper while handling. Because most varieties have shallow roots, a shallow pot with good drainage will work well. Fertilize during the spring and early summer, and you will be rewarded with flowers that usually grow in bright colors from the tops of the plants.

Care and propagation: Many cacti are easily propagated by cutting offsets that grow at the plant's base. Allow the tip of the cutting to dry and callus for a few days before planting.

Common pests and diseases: Pests to look for in your cacti include thrips, mealybugs, spider mites, scale insects, and aphids. Be careful not to over-water cacti because it can cause root rot. Be careful of bruises or injury to your cactus, as bruised areas are susceptible to disease. A natural aging process causes what is known as corking; the skin of a cactus will start to turn brown and rough, from the base up. There is nothing wrong with such a plant. If this happens from the top down or in spots in the middle of the plant, however, it is likely sunburn or spider mites, not corking.

Other points of interest: The popularity of cacti comes from the fact that they are so easy to grow and often require little maintenance. It is important to keep cacti away from animals and children to protect them from the spines. If spines become stuck in your skin, try sticking heavy-duty tape on the spines to pull them out. Larger spines may need to be removed with tweezers. Note that it is illegal to harvest wild cacti from desert areas of North America and transport them elsewhere. Buy your plants from a reputable dealer.

Cast iron plant

Common names: Cast iron plant, iron plant

Botanical name: *Aspidistra elatior*

Plant description: The cast iron plant gets its name from its ability to live in even the harshest conditions. This is an excellent plant for a beginning houseplant gardener because it can withstand a level of neglect or mistakes that would damage other plants. The plant, a native of China, has dark green, sword-shaped leaves that can grow from 12 to 20 inches long. Some varieties have white streaks or dots along the leaves. The insignificant flowers grow near the bottom of the plant and are difficult to see. The leathery leaves grow vertically from the root ball.

Light requirements: The cast iron plant grows in virtually all conditions and will thrive in a sunny or semi-sunny window as well as low-light windows. Make sure the plant is not placed in direct sun, and if you move it between different light conditions, introduce it to the new environment slowly so it will have time to adjust. Low-light conditions are ideal for this plant, but it will manage to survive in higher amounts of light.

Temperature and humidity: This plant can tolerate most growing conditions, from burning heat to near frost temperatures, or from low to high humidity.

Watering: Water the plant as the soil begins to dry out, but be sure that the soil does not become too soggy or too hard.

Soil and fertilizing: Cast iron plants can survive in a variety of soils, but the ideal soil is a mix of one part peat moss to one part potting soil. Variegated varieties tend to lose their color patterns if the soil is too rich. The plant should be fertilized only during the growing season, and then with a diluted mixture of a balanced fertilizer.

Care and propagation: Propagate the cast iron plant by dividing clumps after the active growing season, when the plant starts to go dormant. The divisions should be potted a little deeper than the original clump.

Common pests and diseases: If this plant becomes waterlogged, it will become susceptible to root rot. Suspect pests for the cast iron plant include scale insects, mealybugs, and spider mites.

Other points of interest: If your houseplant becomes too large, you can slowly acclimate it to the yard and then plant it in a shady location. This plant is grown as an outdoor shade plant in growing zones of 7 to 10 feet.

Chinese evergreen

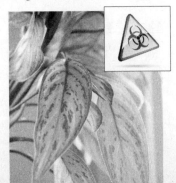

Common name(s): Chinese evergreen, silver queen, poison dart plant

Botanical name: *Aglaonema commutatum*

Plant description: Chinese evergreens are plants from the rainforests of eastern Asia. The plant has leaves that are sword-like or shaped like narrow ovals and are usually dark to medium green. Some species have cream-colored markings along the leaf veins. The plant produces a few small, pale green flowers at a time, and sometimes the flowers produce red berries.

Light requirements: It can tolerate some neglect or less-than-ideal conditions, but its ideal environment is low light near a north or east window.

Temperature and humidity: For the Chinese evergreen, 65 to 75 degrees is the optimal temperature range, with average to high humidity.

Watering: Keep the soil evenly moist, and avoid overwatering this plant under low light conditions.

Soil and fertilizing: Chinese evergreens prefer heavy soil, such as a mixture of two parts potting soil to one part crushed clay. Keep the soil moist but not soggy.

Care and propagation: The Chinese evergreen prefers dry air the most, but it will benefit from regular misting when indoor air is dry. This plant can be propagated through stem cuttings, air layering, or root division.

Common pests and diseases: Keep an eye out for mealybugs, scale insects, and aphids. Waterlogged soil will cause root rot in this plant.

Other points of interest: Note that the sap of this plant is poisonous. It can irritate your skin on contact and will irritate your mouth, lips, throat, and tongue if swallowed.

Coleus

Common name(s): Coleus, flame nettle, painted nettle

Botanical name: *Solenostemon scutellarioids*

Plant description: Coleus plants have highly colored foliage on oval leaves with pointed tips and scalloped edges. These plants come in a surprising variety of colors and variegations, from deep purple to lime green to cream. The tender, fleshy stems often have tiny hairs growing on them. Plants grow upright, but stems can be pinched off to encourage bushiness. In ideal conditions, coleus will produce spikes full of tiny white or lavender flowers shaped like bells. Clip these spikes as the flowers start to fade or the plant will go into a decline.

Light requirements: When grown indoors, the colors will become brighter with more exposure to sunlight.

Temperature and humidity: Coleus is often grown as an outdoor annual, but the slightest frost will kill them. Most species thrive in temperatures between 60 and 80 degrees.

Watering: Keep evenly moist. Water when the surface of the soil feels dry.

Soil and fertilizing: Pot the plants in a light, all-purpose potting soil.

Care and propagation: The leaves will grow well if given a gentle, luke-warm shower several times a year. Plants will develop brown leaf edges if allowed to dry out. These plants root quickly when stem cuttings are placed in water. Sometimes the cuttings will develop different colors and variegation patterns than the original plant.

Common pests and diseases: Mealybugs, aphids, and whiteflies are particular dangers for coleus, so treat these pests aggressively if found.

Other points of interest: This is one of the most colorful houseplants because of the variegated leaf colors. Coleus can easily take the place of a blooming plant to quickly add a burst of color. Low light causes spindly growth for this plant. Once it blooms, the plant tends to lose its color and vigorous growth habits.

Croton

Common name(s): Croton, Joseph's coat

Botanical name: *Codiaeum variegatum*

Plant description: Crotons are brightly colored tropical plants that are native to the Caribbean. The plants grow on a main tough, woody stem, though root balls may develop many stems. The oval-shaped, leathery leaves display splotches of bright yellow, red, green, purple, and orange. The leaves often have a glossy sheen; keep them shiny by wiping the leaves with a wet cloth twice a month.

Light requirements: Crotons prefer bright light.

Temperature and humidity: Crotons like moderate humidity and a warm, 60- to 85-degree environment. Avoid cold drafts.

Watering: Keep the soil slightly moist all the time, and mist regularly during the winter.

Soil and fertilizing: The plant will begin to drop leaves if the soil is too dry. Fertilize the plant with a full-strength general-purpose fertilizer once a month.

Care and propagation: Mist the plants occasionally, and water when the topsoil is dry. Propagate through air layering or stem cuttings.

Common pests and diseases: Mealybugs are a common resident on crotons. Also look for spider mites and scale insects.

Other points of interest: The croton is a poisonous plant that will irritate the mouth and digestive tract if eaten. The colors on the leaves of crotons become more intense if the plant receives plenty of direct sunlight.

Dragontree

Common name(s): Dragontree, corn plant, rainbow plant, song of India, luck bamboo, ribbon plant

Botanical name: *Dracaena spp.*

Plant description: Dragontrees grow tough, sword-shaped leaves from woody trunks or directly from the root crown in an upright growth habit. These leaves can be dark or light green, or they may have yellow, red, or white stripes along the leaf edges. Dragontrees are tropical plants that can grow quite large in the wild, but young, small plants can be kept to windowsill size by limiting their pot size and pruning.

Light requirements: Dragontrees grow best in medium light with no direct sunlight. The coloring of striped leaves will become more intense in plants exposed to more sunlight.

Temperature and humidity: Keep dragontrees out of cold drafts. This species prefers an average room temperature of 65 to 75 degrees.

Watering: Provide the plant with a thorough watering, and then let the soil become somewhat dry before the next watering.

Soil and fertilizing: Pot dragontrees in all-purpose gardening soil with some added peat moss, and fertilize on a monthly basis with a commercial fertilizer.

Care and propagation: Old plants can become leggy and develop tough, woody stems; prune back to foster new growth. Rinse the leaves once or twice a year in a gentle, lukewarm shower to wash away dust and debris. Dragontrees can be propagated through air layering.

Common pests and diseases: The plant is especially vulnerable to scale, mealybugs, and spider mites. To avoid root rot, do not overwater.

Other points of interest: Dracaenas are grown for the striking color of their leaves and are ideal plants for decorating living areas and offices.

Dumbcane

Common name(s): Dumbcane, spotted dumbcane

Botanical name: *Dieffenbachia spp.*

Plant description: Dumbcane comes from tropical South America. It grows vertical stems with sword-shaped, variegated leaves in many colors, including white, cream, and dark or light green. Some varieties of this plant species can grow up to several feet tall; on a windowsill garden, limit its growth through pot size and pruning. As the plant grows, it will shed lower leaves to reveal the colorful stem.

Light requirements: Dumbcane is another popular houseplant that adapts well to filtered, semi-sunny or low-light windows. These leaves will develop burn marks and begin to wilt if exposed to direct sunlight.

Temperature and humidity: This plant prefers average to warm temperatures between 65 and 80 degrees with moderate humidity. Do not place dumbcane plants in a cold, drafty area.

Watering: Keep soil lightly moist, but do not waterlog.

Soil and fertilizing: It grows best in a balanced potting soil and a pot with good drainage. Keep the soil uniformly moist. If the soil becomes dry, the plant will wilt and form brown edges on each leaf. Too much water will make the plant's leaves yellow and floppy. This plant will benefit from a full-strength fertilizer once a month.

Care and propagation: Propagate new plants through stem cuttings or air layering.

Common pests and diseases: Dumbcane is susceptible to mealybugs and spider mites.

Other points of interest: All parts of this plant are poisonous. It can cause irritation and swelling to your mouth, lips, throat, and tongue if swallowed; it also can cause breathing problems. The sap is particularly poisonous to cats, so they should not be allowed to play with the leaves. Dumbcane plants adapt easily to most homes and offices.

English ivy

Common name(s): English ivy

Botanical name: *Hedera helix*

Plant description: English ivy is an evergreen vine with dark green or variegated leathery leaves that are heart-shaped or deeply lobed with three to five points. This vine is a popular European plant that has been transplanted to North America. It is grown outdoors as well as indoors and can be seen climbing old houses and walls or used as a ground cover. When grown outdoors, it turns reddish-orange in the winter and produces flowers and poisonous berries in the summer. It is difficult to get indoor ivy to bloom, though.

Light requirements: This plant can live in any light condition, from bright, filtered sunlight to low light. Ideal temperatures range from 50 to 70 degrees.

Temperature and humidity: The ivy can tolerate high or low temperatures but does not do well in constant hot or cold drafts.

Watering: Allow the surface of the soil to dry between waterings, but do not let the soil dry out completely because the plant will begin to drop leaves. English ivy will benefit from frequent misting.

Soil and fertilizing: Plant ivy in a well-balanced soil mixture, and keep the soil evenly moist. This plant does not require additional fertilizing unless the soil is poor, but it can benefit from a balanced fertilizer every month or two.

Care and propagation: You can grow ivy as a long vine, pinch the vines back to encourage the growth of more vines, or clip the plant into any shape you desire. As the plant ages, the stems may grow hard and woody, and you may want to clip a cutting and start new plants. The vines themselves will produce new roots into the soil if allowed sufficient space, and stem cuttings will develop new roots quickly.

Common pests and diseases: English ivy is especially susceptible to spider mites, which can cause the growth of undersized leaves of reddish or brownish color. The plant can also suffer from problems with aphids, mealybugs, and scale insects, as well as diseases like bacterial spot, stem rot, and fungal leaf spots.

Other points of interest: English ivy is one of the most common houseplants. One enjoyable trait of English ivy is its ability to be shaped and twined around supports. This plant climbs by producing strong root-like suckers that can be difficult to remove once entrenched. Ivy is a toxic plant; its sap can cause skin irritation, and eating any part of the plant will cause stomach upset.

Fern

Plant description: Ferns have been consistently popular houseplants since gardeners began bringing them indoors. They are easy to grow, require little care, and do an outstanding job of purifying indoor air. There are dozens of types of ferns, with foliage that ranges from delicate, feathery fronds to stiff, dramatic fans of foliage. Some ferns, such as the painted lady, are variegated with silver and purple, but most ferns range in color from light to dark green. Ferns that are often grown successfully as houseplants include:

- **Maidenhair fern** (*Adiantum pedatum*) — Maidenhair ferns require high humidity, so they are ideal candidates for a terrarium. They can be distinguished by their prominent black, hair-like stalks with small, broad, frilly leaves.

- **Bird's nest fern** (*Asplenium nidus*) — The bird's nest fern is an easy plant to grow indoors with a relatively high humidity. However, this particular species is not easy to propagate. It is an unusual-looking fern, having scalloped leaves that droop over into a fountain-like structure.

- **Brazilian treefern** (*Blechnum moorei*) — The Brazilian treefern is a popular fern variety from the Victorian era. It has a small trunk and grows in a rosette shape. Its fronds are crinkled or ruffled. New fronds will be a bright red color. Although it grows slowly, it thrives in home environments with little care.

- **Treefern** (*Cyathea spp.*) — The treefern is a slow-growing plant with fronds that can reach 10 feet when it lives in a high humidity environment. In drier environments, the fronds only grow to about 2 to 4 feet. This fern is best purchased already full-grown so you can immediately enjoy its tree stature.

- **Japanese hollyfern** (*Cyrtomium falcatum*) — Japanese hollyfern is one of the most tolerate indoor ferns. This plant is known by its deep green fronds with small leaves that are shaped like holly leaves. Unlike a lot of ferns, the Japanese hollyfern does not shed. It is a slow-growing plant that may reach 2 feet in width over time.

- **Rabbit's foot fern** (*Davallia spp.*) — The rabbit's foot fern is a popular and traditional houseplant. It is also known as the squirrel foot's or deer foot's fern because of its finely divided fronds and furry rhizomes. A slow grower, this plant requires minimal care and prefers small pots, making it an ideal candidate for a windowsill.

- **Boston swordfern** (*Nephrolepis exaltata*) — A popular variety for homes, the Boston swordfern has frilly, bright-green leaves and long hanging fronds. This fern is also known as fluffy ruffles. A species that originated in Africa, the Boston swordfern is tolerant of many indoor conditions.

Although ferns appear to be delicate plants because of their fine leaves and flexible branches, they are a popular choice for houseplants — especially windowsills.

Light requirements: Ferns grow best in moderate light, and some varieties can be severely damaged by exposure to direct sunlight.

Temperature and humidity: These plants appreciate moderate to cooler temperatures, and the leaves will quickly turn brown if exposed to drafts of hot, dry air. Ferns appreciate high humidity, so they are good candidates for terrariums and are also perfect for growing alongside other humidity-loving plants like bromeliads, African violets, or orchids.

Watering: It is best to water when the top inch or two of soil is dried out.

Soil and fertilizing: The most important factor in keeping ferns healthy is to keep the soil consistently moist and provide a sufficient amount of humidity. If the fern is allowed to dry out, it will wilt and drop leaves. Ferns thrive in a peaty soil that is slightly acidic.

Care and propagation: Mist the plant with cool water each week. Ferns propagate through spores, which can be difficult for the home gardener, but you can also create new plants by dividing the root ball of healthy, mature plants.

Common pests and diseases: Mealybugs, spider mites, and scale insects are all possible pests for ferns.

Other points of interest: The root ball grows close to the surface in most varieties, so be careful not to disturb it or accidentally tip the plant out of its pot. Some types of ferns will grow in an aquaculture garden as well. Ferns are sensitive to pesticides and tobacco smoke. However, when you have a fern that is in excellent health, it is a good indicator that the surrounding air is clean and uncontaminated.

Ficus

Common name(s): Weeping fig, fiddle-leaf fig, rubber plant, creeping fig

Botanical name: *Ficus spp.*

Plant description: Ficus plants have been well-loved houseplants for decades. They come from tropical areas around the world and have religious significance to Buddhists. Many indoor gardeners have taller tree specimens, but young, small plants can be kept undersized by limiting their pot size and pruning. Ficus trees are excellent candidates for training to a standard or groomed as bonsai plants, and the trunks can actually be braided or trained to unusual shapes. There are also dwarf varieties that are perfect for a windowsill or terrarium garden. Ficus plants grow from either one central, woody trunk or numerous small woody stems. The leaves are usually sword-shaped or almond-shaped and have a glossy green color that can be enhanced by wiping the leaves with a wet cloth from time to time. Some types have a red or brown blush to the central vein of each leaf.

Light requirements: The best environment for a ficus is a semi-sunny window or a filtered sunny window, but the ficus is a versatile plant; it can also do well with shady spots, but the leaves will not be as plentiful and the branches will grow thin and weepy.

Temperature and humidity: The plant grows well in the normal household temperature range of 60 to 85 degrees. It will drop leaves and branches if exposed to drafts or room temperatures below 55 degrees.

Watering: Too little water will also cause it to lose foliage, as will moving the plant around.

Soil and fertilizing: Plant the ficus in a mixture of garden soil and peat, and keep the plant evenly moist, especially in the summer. Provide half-strength all-purpose fertilizer every two weeks during the growing season, but refrain from feeding during the dormant season.

Care and propagation: Ficus can be propagated through stem tip cuttings of non-woody branches or by air layering.

Common pests and diseases: Unfortunately, this plant variety is susceptible to many insect pests, including mites, mealybugs, whiteflies, and aphids.

Other points of interest: All specimens have a growing season when they produce many new leaves and branches, followed by a resting season.

Grape ivy

Common name(s): Grape ivy, oakleaf ivy, kangaroo vine, begonia vine

Botanical name: *Cissus rhombifolia* or *Cissus alata*

Plant description: Grape ivy is a vining plant that grows wild in the West Indies and South America. It climbs by attaching to

supports with small curling tendrils. The plant grows glossy, compound leaves with three leaflets that look like small grape leaves; the color ranges from dark to medium green. Grape ivy's stems are covered with soft, brown hair.

Light requirements: Grape ivy is a tolerant, easy-to-grow plant that does well in low to medium filtered light.

Temperature and humidity: Grape ivy is easy to grow in a temperature range from 60 to 85 degrees.

Watering: Water the plant when the soil is dry, and make sure the saucer does not retain any standing water.

Soil and fertilizing: It requires a balanced potting soil, preferably African violet soil, and good drainage, because it tends to rot in overly moist soil. Apply half-strength balanced fertilizer to the plant every three months.

Care and propagation: This plant will benefit from occasional misting. The plant can be easily shaped by clipping vines and can be propagated through stem clippings.

Common pests and diseases: Watch for whiteflies, mealybugs, and spider mites. Grape ivy is also susceptible to powdery mildew, which can be hard to control once it has infested the plant.

Other points of interest: Known for its climbing nature, grape ivy is generally grown in hanging baskets or trained to climb trellises. This plant grows rapidly in home environments and is popular in office environments. Grape ivy is the most durable plant in the Cissus species.

Jade plant

Common name(s): Jade plant, airplane plant, baby jade, moss crassula, rattail crassula, rattlesnake, scarlet-paintbrush, silver jade plant

Botanical name: *Crassula ovata*

Plant description: The jade plant is a succulent plant that grows thick, fleshy oval leaves on thick stems that become woody in old age. Jade plants are generally dark green in color, but there are also light green and red-tipped varieties. These plants are long-lived and can be trained as bonsai plants or simply trimmed in interesting shapes. Older plants can grow to 4 or 5 feet tall with numerous branches.

Light requirements: As a desert plant, jade plants thrive in direct sun but expose the plant gradually so that it can adjust to the sunlight. It will also grow (albeit more slowly) in medium or low-light windows.

Temperature and humidity: Jade plants can thrive in temperatures ranging from cool to hot. They prefer an average room temperature of 65 to 70 degrees year-round. Jade plants prefer low to average humidity.

Watering: Let the soil dry out to about half the pot's topsoil before watering. Jade plants that are watered too often will become yellow and squishy, especially around the leaves, causing the plant to rot. When a jade plant is receiving too little water, it will usually turn a darker color and appear to shrink in on itself. It will quickly recover unless it is so damaged that it begins to brown.

Soil and fertilizing: It prefers soil with equal parts peat moss, gardening soil, and sand. Jade plants have shallow roots, so be sure to tamp down the soil around the plants so that they do not topple over before the roots take hold. Fertilize the plant once a month with all-purpose fertilizer.

Care and propagation: You can easily keep the jade plant to the size of your windowsill by pinching off new growth. Rinse the leaves once or twice a year in a gentle, lukewarm shower to clean them of dust and debris. You can also propagate these plants by rooting leaf cuttings. The plant readily produces new plantlets that can be planted in a new pot.

Common pests and diseases: Mealybugs are a particular problem with jade plants. Get rid of these pests by dabbing each bug with a cotton swab dipped in rubbing alcohol, and then wipe the leaves of the plant with clean water to remove as much of the alcohol as possible. You may have to repeat this process several times before all the bugs are killed, as they can be difficult to eliminate.

Other points of interest: This popular plant is easy to grow in homes and offices. If you are not familiar with the botanical name, check *Crassula argentea*, its former name.

Ming aralia

Common name(s): Ming aralia, aralia, parsley aralia

Botanical name: *Polyscias fruticosa*

Plant description: The ming aralia is an exotic-looking shrub from the South Pacific. The deeply divided leaves grow on gracefully drooping stems, and on older, larger plants, the plant will develop a center trunk and woody branches. These leaves often have a glossy sheen; keep them shiny by wiping the leaves with a wet cloth from time to time.

Light requirements: This plant grows best in a sunny window, but without exposure to direct sunlight. On a sunny windowsill, a small specimen can be placed in the shade of a larger plant that appreciates direct sunlight and will thus be protected from receiving too much sun.

Temperature and humidity: Medium to high humidity and average temperatures are best for this plant.

Watering: This is an easy to care for plant if you make sure you water it properly. The plant must be kept moist all the time, but do not let the soil become soggy or allow the pot to sit in a saucer of water.

Soil and fertilizing: Pot the plant in a soil mix of one part garden soil, one part coarse sand or perlite, and one part peat moss.

Care and propagation: It will benefit from occasional misting. Propagate new plants by taking stem cuttings that can be rooted directly in new soil.

Common pests and diseases: Check aralias regularly for spider mites, mealybugs, and scale insects. Do not overwater as this leads to stem rot.

Other points of interest: Aralia can grow up to 8 feet tall but can easily be pruned or even trained into interesting shapes. Ming aralia is often grown as a popular bonsai plant.

Norfolk Island pine

Common name(s): Norfolk Island pine

Botanical name: *Araucaria heterophylla*

Plant description: The Norfolk Island pine is an evergreen tree that is native to the South Pacific. In the wild, it grows in thick groves, but as a houseplant, it is a slow-growing, long-lived potted plant. Buy the right size for your window, and it will take years before it outgrows its space. From its needled trunk, graceful fans of branches grow with soft, medium to dark green needles. The pine has specific, exact requirements, so it is not a plant for beginning gardeners or those with little time to care for it.

Light requirements: This plant grows best in the moderate light of a semi-sunny window. Turn the plant occasionally to make sure all sides grow evenly. It will suffer from exposure to direct sun or extremes in temperature; needle and branch loss will result.

Temperature and humidity: It thrives in cooler temperatures; ideally, the plant should be in a room between 60 and 70 degrees that is slightly cooler at night. The most important factor in keeping a Norfolk Island pine healthy is consistently moist soil and a good amount of humidity. If the pine is allowed to dry out, it will drop needles and branches, and these will not regenerate.

Watering: Water this pine when the top inch or two of soil has dried out.

Soil and fertilizing: Pot it in moist, well-draining general potting soil, find an ideal spot for this small tree, and take care with its watering needs.

Care and propagation: Mist the plant with cool water each week. Do not prune the tree except to remove dead branches or browned tips. Any parts of the tree will not grow back, and unlike many plants, you cannot encourage the plant to grow bushier by pruning the tips. It is difficult for a home gardener to propagate this plant.

Common pests and diseases: Spider mites, mealybugs, and scale insects can create problems for this plant.

Other points of interest: Its evergreen appearance makes it a great replacement for a Christmas tree, especially in smaller living spaces. For a fuller-looking evergreen, plant several seedlings in the same pot.

Peperomia

Common name(s): Watermelon peperomia, Baby rubber plant

Botanical name: *Peperomia spp.*

Plant description: Peperomia is a genus with many different varieties, making it an interesting plant collector's project. Generally, the small, bushy plant has oval or roundish leaves on thin stems. These leaves can be wrinkled, deeply grooved along the veins, or smooth; most leaves are glossy, but a few are waxy. Peperomia plants come in all sorts of colors and variegations, including dark green, red, dark purple, burgundy, gray, cream, or silver. Because of their small size, you can group several in a windowsill garden.

Light requirements: Most peperomias require low to moderate light from an east or north window. You can also use a bright fluorescent light.

Temperature and humidity: These plants were transported from tropical South America and enjoy moderate temperatures from 65 to 75 degrees. They are sensitive to the amount of humidity in the air and the moisture in the soil. The room's humidity should be between 40 and 50 percent. Peperomia plants are ideal for terrariums.

Watering: Allow the soil to dry slightly before watering again.

Soil and fertilizing: The plant thrives in light African violet soil, but care must be taken so that it does not dry out completely or become over-moist.

Care and propagation: As the plant ages, it may create vines. Pinch back new growth to encourage bushiness. Peperomias propagate easily through step cuttings or leaf tips, so there are plenty to share with friends.

Common pests and diseases: Potential pests for peperomias are mealy-bugs, scale insects, and spider mites. These plants are susceptible to corky scab, crown rot, or oedema if overwatered.

Other points of interest: Because of its easy-care nature, peperomias make ideal plants for the workplace. Peperomias are known for their dazzling foliage and range of shapes, textures, and colors.

Philodendron

Common name(s): Lacy-tree philodendron, anchor philodendron, bushing philodendron, climbing philodendron, heartleaf philodendron

Botanical name: *Philodendron spp.*

Plant description: Philodendrons are another common houseplant, and part of their appeal is their easy care requirements. These plants grow thick, fleshy vines with large, glossy, heart-shaped leaves; they range in color from dark green, variegated cream, blue-green, lime green, and yellow. Some varieties have deeply lobed leaves that look like the leaves of oak trees.

Light requirements: You often see these plants in offices because they adapt to many lighting conditions, even total fluorescent light with no sunlight. They grow equally well in low light as in filtered bright sunshine, though the coloring will become more intense in plants exposed to more sunlight.

Temperature and humidity: Average to warm temperatures ranging from 60 to 80 degrees will create the best atmosphere for this plant. Most philodendrons grow best in average humidity, but a few species prefer high humidity.

Watering: A philodendron thrives when you provide a thorough watering and then let the soil become somewhat dry before the next watering.

Soil and fertilizing: Pot the plant in average, loamy soil and fertilize on a monthly basis. In fact, philodendrons can actually survive without any soil — simply place a stem cutting in a vase or glass of water, and provide a diluted fertilizer every other month to grow it hydroponically.

Care and propagation: Most varieties of philodendron can grow quite large, so if you do not plan to provide support for the vines or allow them to cascade off the windowsill, you may want to trim back the new growth from time to time. A small pot may not limit the growth of the plant, but rather force it to grow single large leaves on one stem. The plant propagates easily from stem cuttings but can also be increased through air layering.

Common pests and diseases: Philodendrons are usually pest-free, but spider mites, mealybugs, and scale insects are possible pests.

Other points of interest: Philodendrons are long-lived and easy to grow. They have an excellent ability to remove pollutants from the air. All parts of the plant are toxic, and the sap will irritate the skin.

Ponytail palm

Common name(s): Ponytail palm, bottle palm, elephant foot

Botanical name: *Beaucarnea recurvata*

Plant description: The ponytail plant has long, narrow leaves that hang down, giving it a cascading look. The leaves grow out from the thick, palm-like stem. Because the leaves droop down, the ponytail plant can be grown in a hanging pot until it gets too large. Though this plant looks similar to a palm, it is actually a relative of the lily family. It may also be referred to as a bottle palm because of the thick stem or trunk, or an elephant foot tree. The ponytail palm is native to desert Mexico. This plant has a slow growth rate. Even though it can get quite large, it will take a long time to do so. Select a small specimen for your windowsill, and control growth through pot size.

Light requirements: Being a desert plant, it does well in bright, sunny areas like a windowsill.

Temperature and humidity: The warm, dry air of the house is a good growing condition for this plant. It grows best in temperate ranging from 65 to 75 degrees. Due to its natural preference for warm and dry conditions, it develops a root system similar to cacti.

Watering: The soil on the top quarter of the pot should be dry before re-watering. Watering every one to two weeks should be more than enough for this plant.

Soil and fertilizing: Because this plant mimics a cactus, cactus potting soil would be ideal. Make sure it is fast-draining soil. In the spring and summer, fertilize with a balanced houseplant fertilizer, and do not feed in the winter.

Care and propagation: Ponytail palms have a finicky watering requirement. Take care not to overwater this plant, particularly in the winter. Ponytail palms tend to collect dust, so a mid-winter misting and a soft cloth to clean off the leaves should be all this plant requires.

Common pests and diseases: When overwatered, ponytail palms will exhibit stem rot or bacterial soft rot caused by fungi and bacteria, respectively. Spider mites are the common pest to look for on this plant.

Other points of interest: Ponytail palms are wonderful long-term companions. Once you figure out their water requirements, they are easy to please. The bulbous shape of this plant's lower trunk classifies it as a semi-succulent. This is where it keeps its water reserves.

Pothos

Common name(s): Pothos, devil's ivy

Botanical name: *Epipremnum aureum*

Plant description: Pothos and philodendron can some-

times be mistaken for each other. Pothos, also called devil's ivy, is also a vining plant with glossy, heart-shaped leaves; they range in color from dark green, variegated cream, blue-green, lime green, and yellow. Pothos has varieties with smaller leaves that may be more suitable for a windowsill garden. Pothos generally has more slender, flexible vines than a philodendron.

Light requirements: Pothos is an easy-to-grow vining plant that can thrive in a variety of lighting conditions, from complete artificial light to sunny windows. However, direct sunlight can burn the leaves.

Temperature and humidity: Pothos likes average temperature between 60 and 80 degrees with an average humidity level.

Watering: This plant is extremely hardy, and you can let it dry out before watering again.

Soil and fertilizing: It will grow well in almost any soil, except dense, hard, or acidic soil.

Care and propagation: Keep the leaves glossy by wiping them with a wet cloth occasionally. It is also a good candidate for a hydroponic, or soilless, garden. If the plant is kept in a small pot, it will adjust to conditions by producing smaller leaves and stems. Promote bushiness by snipping off new growth, or provide support if you would like to allow it to climb. The plant propagates easily from stem cuttings but can also be increased through air layering.

Common pests and diseases: Possible pests for the pothos plant are spider mites and scale insects. Be careful not to overwater as this can cause root rot.

Other points of interest: Pothos has the understandable reputation for being the easiest houseplant to grow. Vigorous and fast growers, pothos plants make the perfect low-maintenance plant for homes and offices. These plants are known for their air purifying properties, however, pothos has poisonous — but non-lethal — sap, which can cause a burning sensation in the mouth if eaten.

Prayer plant

Common name(s): Prayer plant, cathedral windows, rabbit tracks

Botanical name: *Maranta leuconeura*

Photo By Angela Williams Duea

Plant description: The prayer plant gets its name from its habit of folding up its leaves lengthwise at dark, resembling hands folded in prayer. The profuse foliage is dark to medium green with red, brown, maroon, black, yellow, or pink patches — or marks of several different colors — in a regular pattern between the cross-veins on each leaf. All varieties have a bushy, mounded growing habit.

Light requirements: All varieties grow well in bright, indirect sun or semi-sunny locations.

Temperature and humidity: It thrives in high humidity, and smaller varieties are good candidates for a terrarium.

Watering: The soil should be allowed to dry out slightly before watering again, but lack of water will cause the leaf tips to brown.

Soil and fertilizing: The plant thrives in rich, well-drained soil with added peat moss for good drainage. Fertilize this plant every two weeks with a diluted all-purpose fertilizer.

Care and propagation: The leaves will grow well if rinsed once or twice a year in a gentle, lukewarm shower. Prayer plants can be propagated through root divisions or leaf cuttings.

Common pests and diseases: Be careful of spider mites, scale insects, and root mealybugs with this plant. Do not overwater prayer plants because this will lead to root rot.

Other points of interest: Some varieties of this plant are called cathedral windows because they resemble the arches of stained glass windows. Other varieties are called rabbit tracks because of the interesting markings on the oval or rounded leaves, which look like small paw prints or long arrow-heads.

Snake plant

Common name(s): Snake plant, mother-in-law's tongue

Botanical name: *Sansevieria trifasciata*

Plant description: The snake plant is a native of Africa. It gets its name from the upright, stiff, blade-shaped leaves that grow directly from the root rhizome; the edges of these leaves can be sharp. Some of the smaller, compact cultivars are ideal for a shady windowsill, but the most common varieties can grow several feet tall. Snake plants are dark green or gray-green with yellow, white, or cream-colored stripes, especially along the edges of each leaf; some plants have vertical stripes of one color and horizontal stripes of another color.

Light requirements: This plant enjoys bright indirect light from spring through fall and moderate light in the winter. Snake plants actually do not grow well in dark corners and total aridity.

Temperature and humidity: Snake plants prefer average temperatures between 65 and 75 degrees with a low to average humidity level.

Watering: It has minimal watering needs, especially in winter, when you may only need to water it once a month. The rhizome will easily rot if the plant is overwatered.

Soil and fertilizing: Pot this plant in a mixture of one part sand to two parts soil, and after thoroughly watering, allow it to dry out completely before watering again.

Care and propagation: To propagate, divide the rhizomes and plant in rooting medium.

Common pests and diseases: Check this plant periodically for spider mites and mealybugs. Do not overwater because this can lead to root rot.

Other points of interest: If you are looking for a carefree houseplant, look no further than the snake plant — a great plant for beginners. Because of its easily adaptable nature, the snake plant is ideal for homes, workplaces, and even shopping malls. This plant has an excellent ability to remove pollutants from the air.

Spider plant

Common name(s): Spider plant, airplane plant

Botanical name: *Chlorophytum comosum*

Plant description: Spider plants get their name from the little plantlets that grow from long stems dropping down the sides of the "mother" plant; these little plants look like spiders dropping from a web. The leaves are narrow and strap-like, and they range in color from dark to light green, some with a white streak down the center of the leaf. The plant also produces white flowers throughout the year.

Light requirements: Spider plants can thrive in almost any environment, though the colors will be the brightest in a brighter atmosphere. In sunny locations, keep the plants from exposure to direct sunlight, as this will burn the leaves.

Temperature and humidity: Spider plants like average room temperatures from 65 to 75 degrees. Avoid cool temperatures below 55 degrees and high temperatures above 80 degrees.

Watering: In spring and summer months, keep evenly moist; soaking seems to work the best. For fall and winter, allow the soil's surface to dry before watering again.

Soil and fertilizing: They do not require any special soil requirements other than needing good drainage in the pot. If the soil becomes too dry, the leaves will begin to wither and turn brown at the ends. Feed the plant a half-strength balanced fertilizer four times a year.

Care and propagation: Each dangling plantlet is ready to be transplanted into its own pot when you see brown, somewhat hard adventitious roots budding from the bottom of the "baby." The plantlet can be clipped off the stem and set in water to allow the roots to grow, or it can be placed directly in a new pot. If you do not want to propagate the plant, there is no harm in leaving the draped stems on the main plant.

Common pests and diseases: The only known pests for the spider plant are scale insects.

Other points of interest: Spider plants are popular and easy to grow. This is a great houseplant for beginners, and you can get several new plants from this phenomenally prolific "mother" plant. Spider plants are known for their ability to reduce indoor air pollution.

Umbrella plant

Common name(s): Schefflera, dwarf schefflera, umbrella plant

Botanical name: *Schefflera arboricola*

Plant description: Schefflera, or the umbrella plant, often grows as a large bush, but dwarf varieties are ideal and colorful additions to a windowsill. This plant grows multiple stems that become woody as they mature; clusters of leaves fan out in a rosette, or umbrella shape, from the stems. The foliage is dark green or variegated green and white, with each leaf having a glossy almond shape.

Light requirements: Schefflera can tolerate any lighting condition, from low light to direct sun, but it will thrive and produce plenty of new growth in direct sun. Be careful to introduce the plant slowly to different lighting conditions. Moving too fast from low light to sun will make the leaves tough and dull.

Temperature and humidity: Umbrella plants like average to warm temperatures ranging from 65 to 80 degrees and average humidity levels.

Watering: Water when the topsoil is dry, and mist this plant occasionally. Leaves on this plant will tend to droop when the soil has become too dry.

Soil and fertilizing: Put the plant in a well-rounded mixture of gardening soil, peat moss, and sand, and keep it evenly moist but not wet. The plant will begin to drop leaves if the soil is too dry. Fertilize the plant with a full-strength general-purpose fertilizer once a month.

Care and propagation: Keep the leaves glossy by wiping them with a wet cloth from time to time. The leaves will grow well if rinsed once or twice a year in a gentle, lukewarm shower. The plant can be pruned to maintain a pleasing shape or size. Propagate through air layering or stem cuttings.

Common pests and diseases: The umbrella plant is susceptible to spider mites, thrips, mealybugs, and scale insects. Check this plant every few weeks for these pests. Also be sure not to overwater, which leads to root rot or leaf loss.

Other points of interest: Schefflera can live for a long time, even when given casual care. However, this plant does not bode well when moved often. Moving too frequently causes the schefflera to drop some leaves, so it is best to leave it in one spot as much as possible.

Wandering Jew

Common name(s): Wandering Jew, inch plan, Virginia spiderwort, wandering sailor

Botanical name: *Tradescantia albiflora*

Plant description: Some tradescantia varieties are grown both outdoors and indoors. In the wild, it is a semi-shade woodland plant or tropical-zone vine. This vining plant shows incredible variety in the long oval leaves, growth habit, and stem appearance. The wandering Jew variety grows purple or greenish stems, some with purple hairs, and pointed oval leaves that have a deep central groove and stripes or variegations that range from green to purple to silver. Inch plants produce profuse masses of small green or purple leaves in pointed oval leaves; some types produce small white flowers. Spiderwort can have sword-shaped or strap-like leaves in either green or variegated colors; the foliage can be long and drooping, or small and bushy like the inch plant.

Light requirements: All varieties grow best in bright, indirect sunlight or semi-sunny windows.

Temperature and humidity: These plants perform well in average room temperatures of 60 to 75 degrees. They enjoy high humidity, so they are good candidates for terrariums and are ideal to grow with other humidity-loving plants like bromeliads, ferns, African violets, or orchids. A humidifier may help create the ideal environment. Alternatively, you can place pots in a tray of pebbles that are kept moist enough to generate humidity.

Watering: Good drainage is important because the plants are susceptible to root rot. The plants are also sensitive to under-watering, so consistent, even moisture is necessary. If the pot becomes too dry, the leaves will wilt and then turn brown and crispy; the lower branches will lose their leaves and expose unattractive woody stems with a spray of foliage at the top. Water the plants each time the top inch of soil is nearly dry, and make sure to drain the drip tray an hour after watering so the plant does not stand in water.

Soil and fertilizing: Plant them in a soil mixture of equal parts peat moss and all-purpose gardening soil. Fertilize the plants with a full-strength general-purpose fertilizer every two weeks.

Care and propagating: Cut back any stem that is overly long. This stimulates new growth from the base. Remove dried leaves and pinch stem tips frequently. Propagate new plants from stem cuttings at any time.

Common pests and diseases: The wandering Jew is susceptible to spider mites and aphids. Be careful of root rot, which is often caused by a fungus that may have proliferated in the potting mix.

Other points of interest: The wandering Jew is an extremely easy-to-grow houseplant known for its purple, variegated foliage. This is another plant that is easy to propagate to increase your collection or pass along to friends and family.

Chapter 3

Choosing Flowering Plants for a Splash of Color

Although many plants flower, the flowering plants profiled in this chapter are limited to those grown for their "showy" blooms. This group of plants is often overlooked when considering the ideal candidate for a windowsill. One of the primary reasons is because flowering plants have been known to have special light and humidity requirements. In times past, these plants were often limited to conservatories, greenhouses, and special atriums. However, because of air conditioning systems, temperature regulators, and humidity controllers, flowering plants can now thrive in a home environment. *Chapter 9 explains the various propagation methods, while Chapter 10 discusses the pests and diseases you might come across in detail.*

African violet

Common name(s): African violet

Botanical name: *Saintpaulia wendl*

Plant description: These small plants grow thick, hairy leaves on fleshy stems from a central crown. Some varieties have hairy foliage of purple or leaves rimmed with blush red, but the plant's main attraction is its never-ending sprays of flowers. African violets bloom in blue, purple, lavender, pink, red, white, and multi-colored variations. The flowers can be single, ruffled, fringed, or double-petaled.

Light requirements: They can handle any lighting condition, from indirect, bright sun to medium-low light, but will bloom best in a sunny location. They can become accustomed to direct sunlight by gradually introducing the plant to the sunny location.

Temperature and humidity: The plants grow best in a consistent temperature of 60 to 80 degrees with little variation between day and night temperatures. These plants grow best in a humid environment, so they are good candidates for terrariums and are ideal for growing alongside other humidity-loving plants like bromeliads, ferns, and orchids. A humidifier may help create the ideal environment. Alternatively, you can place the pots in a tray of pebbles that are kept moist enough to generate humidity.

Watering: Keep the plants evenly moist but not waterlogged, as the plants have a tendency to root and stem rot. If water drops on the leaves, the magnifying effect of the sun will burn holes into the leaves, so it is best to supply water by pouring it into the drip tray and allowing it to absorb upward. Water the plants each time the top inch of soil is nearly dry, and make sure to drain the drip tray an hour after watering so the plant does not stand in water.

Soil and fertilizing: The typical African violet soil mix can be bought ready-made, but you can make your own by following the directions in Chapter 7. Fertilize the plants with a half-strength mixture of general-purpose fertilizer every two weeks. During the flowering season, switch to a blend that contains higher levels of phosphorus.

Care and propagation: The foliage and flowers are rather tender and fleshy, and they can break off easily with mishandling. Once a flower begins to fade, pinch it off to encourage more flowers. African violets propagate rapidly through stem tip cuttings or leaf cuttings.

Common pests and diseases: Possible pests that may be found on African violets are cyclamen mites, thrips, aphids, and mealybugs. Diseases that commonly affect African violets include botrytis blight and crown rot.

Other points of interest: These plants used to have a reputation for being finicky and difficult to care for, but they almost take care of themselves once you have set up the proper environment. No other houseplant can stand up to the hardiness and blooms of an African violet, which allows it to thrive indoors for a long time.

Amaryllis

Common name(s): Amaryllis

Botanical name: *Amaryllis*

Plant description: Amaryllis is a bulb plant that is often forced to bloom at Christmas; the festive colors of the large blossoms are a wonderful contrast to the cold or snowy world outside. The large, showy, trumpet-like flowers grow on thick, vertical stems; colors include red, white, or pink, and the petals may also be bicolored. The leaves of the plant are strap-like and dark green. Grown from bulbs, the amaryllis will bloom in six to eight weeks after planting, given the proper conditions.

Light requirements: When the shoots are 4 to 6 inches in length, move the plants to a sunny location.

Temperature and humidity: After watering through, put the pot in a cool location — between 55 and 70 degrees — and watch for the bulbs to produce shoots 4 to 6 inches long.

Watering: Provide even moisture levels but do not let the soil become too soggy because the bulbs will rot easily.

Soil and fertilizing: Put the bulbs in a container of soil mix of one part potting soil, one part sand, and one part perlite or peat moss. Several bulbs can be planted in one pot. Make sure the bulbs are placed so that the top third of the bulb is exposed to air and not farther than 2 inches from the edges of the pot. Provide a balanced, full-strength fertilizer once a week until the plants matures.

Care and propagation: After the blooms die off, cut the stems and allow the bulbs to build up nutrients in a sunny location. Several months after blooming, cut off old leaves and move the pot to a cool, low-light area for ten weeks to three months. During this time, let the soil dry out slightly and discontinue the fertilizing schedule. This will allow the bulbs to rest before beginning the bloom cycle again. Follow the potting and growing instructions to start a new season of blooms. Amaryllis propagates by growing offset bulbs that can be separated from the main bulbs after given a year or so to mature. After this maturation period, break off the new bulbs and plant them in their own pots.

Common pests and diseases: Check the bulbs of the amaryllis to ensure that they are not rotted or hollowed out. If so, then this is a good indicator of narcissus fly infestation. Do not overwater as this leads to root rot.

Other points of interest: This is a commonly used bulb forced to bloom in the wintertime, especially around the holiday season.

Anthurium

Common name(s): Anthurium, flamingo flower

Botanical name: *Anthurium palmatum*

Plant description: Anthurium is a tropical plant with large red bracts and heart-shaped, waxy leaves. The flower bracts make excellent cut flowers and are often seen in florists' arrangements. This plant can grow up to 2 feet tall, but smaller species are more compact and reach a mature height of 9 to 12 inches.

Light requirements: Provide bright to moderate light, but not direct sunlight. The plant begins blooming after the first year and will continue to bloom year-round with plenty of indirect sun. Move the plants to medium-light areas after the flower buds begin to open.

Temperature and humidity: Anthuriums need a consistent temperature of 60 to 85 degrees with little variation between day and night temperatures.

Watering: The plant should be kept evenly moist throughout the spring and summer, and should also be periodically leached of salt accumulation. *Leaching is discussed in Chapter 7.* During the winter, water less often, and then allow the surface to dry completely before the next watering.

Soil and fertilizing: This plant prefers a peaty soil — an African violet mix is ideal. It needs monthly fertilizing with a mix containing extra phosphorus but diluted to quarter strength.

Care and propagation: You can propagate anthuriums once a new crown grows next to the original plant. Pull the crown free and pot in a new container.

Common pests and diseases: Check the soil of anthuriums regularly for fungus gnats. Also look for mealybugs, thrips, and scale insects. Avoid overwatering, which causes root rot.

Other points of interest: Note that anthuriums contain calcium oxalate crystals and toxic proteins. The foliage will produce burning of the mouth if eaten and skin irritation if exposed to the plant's sap. Keep out of reach of children and animals.

Begonia

Common name(s): Begonia

Botanical name: *Begonia spp.*

Plant description: The many varieties of begonias are popular as houseplants and garden annuals. The plants have fleshy, tender foliage in many shapes, variegations, and solid colors. The flowers grow on fleshy yet delicate stems and bloom in a rainbow of colors from yellow to purple. Begonias are ideal windowsill plants because they generally grow to a manageable size and appreciate filtered sunlight. However, begonias require specific environmental conditions to thrive, so these plants will need extra attention in your windowsill garden. Popular outdoor plant varieties

like wax begonias — used as bedding plants — and tuberous begonias —
often grown in hanging planters in semi-shady areas — can be brought inside in the fall. However, there are three main types of begonias cultivated
specifically to be grown as houseplants:

- **Angel-wing begonias** — Angel-wing begonias have lopsided
  leaves with a larger, smooth-edged side and a smaller, serrated side.
  The stems have a graceful drooping habit that can often become
  vine-like, but older stems can grow woody and unattractive. The
  foliage is sometimes spotted with yellow, white, or cream, or it may
  be variegated in the same colors. Some angel-wing begonias have a
  greenish-purple color. The flowers grow in clusters from winter to
  mid-spring.

- **Decorative-leaf begonias** — Begonias with decorative leaves grow
  breathtaking foliage in such a variety that a gardener may become
  tempted to start a collection of different types. Some such plants
  are fancy-leaf begonias, painted-leaf begonias, rex begonias, and
  iron-cross begonias. The foliage is marked with red, purple, pale
  green, silver, or dark green; plants may have variegated leaves, or
  markings along the veins, or leaves with centers of one color and
  an outer circle of another color. The plants have many shapes, too.
  Some grow in a bushy cluster of large heart-shaped leaves, some
  are vining plants, some have small round leaves on upright stems,
  and others have medium-sized roundish leaves growing in a central
  cluster.

- **Winter-blooming begonia** — Winter-blooming begonias are also
  called Reiger hybrids. These plants usually grow as small, bushy
  plants with small, round dark green or red leaves. The tender flowers are shaped like miniature roses in colors ranging from red to

yellow; some flowers are multi-colored with petals that are a blush pink at the stem and fade to yellow at the tips. These plants are often short-lived and may bloom only once, but with extra care, they can be kept for many seasons. No matter the type of begonia you choose, there are some basic needs that are common to all begonias.

Light requirements: They prefer sunny windowsills in the wintertime and indirect sun in the summer. Begonia foliage can be damaged by the heat of direct sun, and the leaves will begin to shrink and become tough.

Temperature and humidity: The plants are sensitive to cold and will wilt easily in cool drafts. The ideal temperature is between 75 and 85 degrees. These plants appreciate high humidity, so they are good candidates for terrariums and are ideal to grow with other humidity-loving plants like bromeliads, ferns, African violets, or orchids. Do not mist these plants because it will encourage the growth of powdery mildew, a particular problem with begonias. A humidifier may help create the ideal environment, or you can place begonia pots in a tray of pebbles that are kept moist enough to generate humidity.

Watering: Begonias grow best in a soil mixture of mostly peat moss with a small amount of all-purpose gardening soil and perlite. Good drainage is important because the plants are susceptible to root rot. The plants are also sensitive to under-watering, so consistent, even moisture is necessary. If the pot becomes too dry, the leaves will wilt and then turn brown and crispy. Lower leaves will shed quickly, and you will be left with long, ugly stems sporting a spray of foliage at the top. Water the plants each time the top inch of soil is nearly dry, and make sure to drain the drip tray an hour after watering so the plant does not stand in water.

Soil and fertilizing: Fertilize the plants with a half-strength mixture of general-purpose fertilizer every two weeks. During the flowering season, switch to a blend that contains higher levels of phosphorus.

Care and propagation: The leaves will grow well if rinsed once or twice a year in a gentle, lukewarm shower. The foliage and flowers are rather tender and fleshy and can break off easily with mishandling. However, begonias are easy to prune, and most varieties will respond with abundant growth. Refrain from pruning during the blooming period because the plant's energy will then be spent in generating new leaves rather than flower buds. Once a flower begins to fade, pinch it off to encourage more flowers. Begonias propagate rapidly through stem tip cuttings or leaf cuttings.

Common pests and diseases: Examine begonias periodically for powdery mildew and mealybugs. Do not overwater because this causes crown rot.

Other points of interest: Although begonias are common outdoor garden plants, they also thrive indoors in bright, warm conditions.

Bromeliad

Common name(s): Bromeliad

Botanical name: *Bromeliaceae spp.*

Plant description: The exotic bromeliad family contains some of the most interesting houseplants a gardener can grow. In the South American rainforests, this family contains species that grow with or without soil in the crevices of plants and the forks of tree branches; some attach to rocks, and some grow down into the forest floor.

Some bromeliads have the ability, unique among plants, to absorb moisture and nutrients directly from the air, while other varieties have leaves that form a central cup to hold water for the plant's moisture needs. Some types can be grown in soilless conditions right in your home. Bromeliads have striking foliage, and all varieties produce flowers. Most types produce thick, tough leaves shaped like swords or ribbons. These leaves may range in color from dark green through pale green, silver, or variegated red. Some leaves have spines along the edges. The plants generally grow in a stiff, rather upright habit, though some types grow in the shape of a bowl. When flowering, the plants first produce a colorful cluster of bracts as smaller, colored leaves, and the flowers come out of the bracts. The bracts and flowers appear in all the colors of the rainbow except blue. Some flower clusters look like the many-petaled Asiatic lilies; others are tiny flowers with short petals and dainty rings of pistils; still others look like large, colorful heads of wheat or palm branches.

Light requirements: These plants can grow in sunny or semi-sunny locations. Plants with stiffer leaves tend to prefer long hours of direct sunlight, while those with softer, more pliable leaves fare better in moderate light conditions. In fact, the tough-leaved plants can thrive on a sunny patio or balcony in the summer, and then should be placed in your windowsill during the winter. If you do move the plant in and out of your house, gradually expose the plant to the new lighting conditions so that the leaves will not be burned and the plant will not suffer from shock.

Temperature and humidity: Bromeliads can thrive in temperatures of 60 to 85 degrees but will suffer at temperatures lower than 60 degrees. All bromeliads thrive when humidity levels are around 50 percent.

Soil and fertilizing: These versatile plants can grow in a small ball of peat moss, nestled in an unusual container such as a hollow in a piece of driftwood or a cradle of netting. In a more conventional pot, mix together one part perlite, one part peat moss, and one part ground bark or chopped pine needles. Bromeliads need excellent drainage and acidic conditions. When potting your plant, bury the roots in a shallow depression. If the roots are planted too deeply, the entire plant could rot. If the plant tends to tip over because of the shallow layer of topsoil, tie it to stakes until the root system takes hold. While they do not require much fertilizer, they will benefit from a diluted all-purpose fertilizer every few weeks during the summer growing season. Rather than pouring the fertilizer solution into the soil, mist the leaves and water reservoir with the mixture.

Care and propagation: Bromeliads store water in their cup reservoirs and may need less watering at the root level than most plants. Make sure you keep the water reservoir filled, and sprinkle the leaves with water as well. Water the soil lightly and make sure the pot drains well. Clear out the water cup every few weeks to ensure the water does not become stagnant or harbor diseases, and rinse the foliage in a gentle, room-temperature shower once a year to remove dust and other debris. Interestingly, any insects that fall into this reservoir will be absorbed as nutrients. Bromeliads are hard to prune back if they become too large. Bromeliads will produce offsets, which can be cut off the main plant when they are about half the size of the original. Plant in a new pot using a partly moist bromeliad soil mix, and keep the new plants in a heavily humid climate until the roots develop. Alternatively, you can cut off the main plant when it begins to decline and allow the offsets to take over the pot.

Common pests and disease: Bromeliads are susceptible to scale insects and mealy bugs.

Other points of interest: Patience is a virtue with bromeliads because they must mature before they can bloom. The varieties of bromeliads grow to varying sizes, so check with the grower to understand which species is best for your windowsill. The plants will not bloom until maturity, and they have a complete life cycle of about three to five years. After the long-lasting blooms have died, many varieties will go into a decline, so it is best to buy a bromeliad before it blooms so you will not have to wait several years for another flowering.

> ***Seed of Knowledge:*** *The most well-known bromeliad is the pineapple.*

Bush lily

Common name(s): Clivia, bush lily

Botanical name: *Clivia miniata*

Plant description: The bush lily is a plant uncommon to many homes but is fairly easy to grow and will reward you with clusters of ten to 20 tubular flowers in orange, pink, yellow, or red. The flowers appear in late winter or early spring after specific environmental adjustments. The plants have a vertical growth habit of strap-like leaves up to 2 feet long, but smaller specimens can be kept in windowsill-sized pots.

Light requirements: Optimal light for this plant is of moderate strength from an east window.

Temperature and humidity: To encourage flowering, the plants need cool temperatures and a dormant season. The plant can be left outside until temperatures drop to 45 or 50 degrees. Make sure you bring the plant inside before a frost. Once indoors, keep it in a cool room — between 55 to 65 degrees.

Watering: Keep evenly moist but water sparingly in the winter. Let the soil dry out before watering again.

Soil and fertilizing: Plant these specimens in a balanced mixture of peat moss and all-purpose gardening soil. Bush lilies should be kept evenly moist throughout the spring and summer and should also be given full-strength fertilizer every two weeks from the beginning of the blooming season to the beginning of the dormant season. During the winter, do not provide any additional nutrients.

Care and propagation: Propagate bush lilies by dividing old plants or repotting the growing crowns of young side plantlets.

Common pests and diseases: Be careful not to overwater as this will cause crown rot.

Other points of interest: Keep in mind that the bush lily has special temperature requirements in order for it to bloom.

Chrysanthemums

Common name(s): Florist's mum, garden mums

Botanical name: *Chrysanthemum spp.*

Plant description: Mums are small, shrub-like plants with small, lobed, dusty green leaves. Bunches of flowers grow in white, yellow, burgundy, rust, maroon, and pink. The leaves and flowers all have a strong, camphor-like odor. Mums are prized in China, where they make tea from the flowers, and the blooms often appear in their art. Most people are familiar with pots of mums flowering in earth-toned puffballs each fall, but chrysanthemums are also a pretty plant in any sunny window. In fact, you may be able to get your pot mum to bloom several times a year by taking it through growth and dormancy periods.

Light requirements: Mums do best in bright sunlight.

Temperature and humidity: Cool to cold temperatures are best for mums. Too high of a temperature causes the flowers to fade.

Watering: They brown easily if they become dried out, so be careful with the watering schedule.

Soil and fertilizing: Plant in a rich, well-drained soil. Fertilize twice a month during the active growing season.

Care and propagation: As the plant blooms begin to fade, cut them off to prolong blooming. At the end of the blooming season, cut the plant back 2 to 3 inches. Put in a shadier spot with cooler temperatures, and refrain from fertilizing. After a period of dormancy, move to a sunny window and begin feeding and watering more heavily again. Plants can be propagated after the blooming season by dividing root sections and planting them in new pots.

Common pests and diseases: These plants easily develop root rot, so do not let them stand in a saucer of water. Mums are susceptible to powdery mildew and anthracnose, a plant disease caused by fungi.

Other points of interest: These plants produce a burst of color and are one of the most affordable flowering plants available. They are known for their ability to remove chemical pollutants from the air indoors.

Cyclamen

Common name(s): Cyclamen, florist's
cyclamen, Persian violet

Botanical name: *Cyclamen persicum*

Plant description: Cyclamens have a
bushy growth habit with oval leaves
speckled with silver and white. The foliage itself is spectacular, but when
the flowers bloom on delicate stems, the plant is gorgeous. The flower petals arch backward from the center of the bloom, and the flowers display
pastel pinks and purples.

Light requirements: Put them on a windowsill that offers moderately filtered light.

Temperature and humidity: Cyclamens prefer cool year-round temperatures from 60 to 70 degrees, but they can tolerate cold as low as 40 degrees.

Watering: Be careful to water often, but do not let the soil become soggy
— the roots will rot quickly.

Soil and fertilizing: Cyclamens are often given as a gift in a foil-wrapped
pot. The foil will hold in moisture and introduce mildew and root rot, so
be sure to remove the packaging and repot the plant in medium-textured
potting soil. Use an all-purpose fertilizer at half-strength every two weeks
during the blooming cycle.

Care and propagation: Once the blooms are spent, clip them to encourage new growth. Yellow leaves will indicate the plant has already gone into
a decline. Propagate through root divisions.

Common pests and diseases: Watch carefully for thrips and spider mites — cyclamens are susceptible to these pests. Treat the plant's diseases aggressively because it will easily succumb to problems.

Other points of interest: Cyclamens have their strongest blooming season during midwinter, providing a lovely accent for indoors. Cyclamens need a specific environment to thrive and will quickly decline in an unhealthy environment. A little extra care is worth it to enjoy the beauty of this plant.

Desert rose

Common name(s): Desert rose

Botanical name: *Adenium obesum*

Plant description: The desert rose is a native of South Africa and has beautiful variations of pink, red, and white flowers. The flowers are much like that of a wild rose. The leaves are green with a glossy appearance, and the stems are thick and lush with a tree-like look. Similar to cacti and the ponytail palm, the base of the trunk becomes thick to retain water in desert conditions. This is a easy plant to raise and keep alive.

Light requirements: It likes the sun and should do well as a windowsill plant.

Temperature and humidity: The desert rose prefers average to high temperatures in general but cool to cold temperatures in the winter. It does well with dry humidity, but it can tolerate humid air.

Watering: It has similar needs as most cacti and should not be overwatered. Allow the soil to dry near the surface before watering again.

Soil and fertilizing: It is best to use a slightly acidic soil blend that is high in peat moss and coarser sand for good drainage. The desert rose does respond well to fertilization. If using plenty of fertilizer, you can water slightly more often as long as the plant is in bright, warm sun. This will promote growth and flowering.

Care and propagation: Seeds are the best way to grow new plants. Branch cutting propagation does not work as well because the base of the stem is usually not thick enough and does not develop well. Seeds germinate best with bright sun and warmth in peat moss that has been sterilized.

Common pests and diseases: This plant can be susceptible to insects, especially aphids. You can use a soap rinse spray to clean it. Do not use insecticides on the desert rose.

Other points of interest: Keep this plant away from house pets. Desert rose sap may be toxic to some house pets.

Flowering maple

Common name(s): Flowering maple, Chinese lantern

Botanical name: *Abutilon hybridum*

Plant description: The flowering maple is not a true maple but gets its name from its wide leaves with five lobes, similar to those of a maple tree. It can grow up to 3 feet tall on a main stem, but the plant can be kept at about half that size and full of bushy branches through regular pruning. This plant produces wide-petaled flowers of orange, yellow, red, or pink; the blossoms look similar to holly-hocks, with five petals and a prominent inner stamen with red pistils.

Light requirements: Flowering maples prefer bright, indirect light from a south or west window.

Temperature: Keep a consistent temperature of 65 to 75 degrees year-round for this plant.

Watering: Water this plant thoroughly, and then allow the surface to dry completely before the next watering.

Soil and fertilizing: Pot the plant in soil containing extra peat, and make sure the pH is slightly acidic. During summer growing months, feed the plant with a balanced fertilizer at full strength every two weeks, but during the dormant winter season, cut back to one feeding per month.

Care and propagation: Prune regularly to maintain bushiness and prevent legginess. Propagate through stem tip cuttings. After a few years, the plants stem may become woody and the leaves may begin to drop from lower limbs. Root new cuttings, and discard the aged plant.

Common pests and diseases: This plant is susceptible to spider mites, aphids, whiteflies, mealybugs, and scale insects, so mist the plant occasionally and make sure the conditions are not too dry.

Other points of interest: The plant will bloom year-round if given adequate fertilizer and sun.

Kalanchoe

Common name(s): Kalanchoe, widow's thrill

Botanical name: *Kalanchoe blossfeldiana*

Plant description: The kalanchoe is a great choice for a flowering houseplant because it is easy to grow and requires minimum care. It is a blooming succulent with green leaves and bunchy beige, yellow, orange, violet, or red flowers that bloom twice a year. This plant is native to Madagascar, but it is cultivated worldwide. The distinguishing flowers can bloom for as long as ten weeks. The average size of a kalanchoe is up to 18 inches tall and 12 inches wide.

Light requirements: Provide bright light for this plant; however, kalanchoes do not like direct sunlight in the summer because the succulent leaves can get sunburned.

Temperature and humidity: Kalanchoes prefer average household temperatures. They are very sensitive to cold, freezing temperatures; therefore, keep the temperature between 65 and 85 degrees.

Soil and fertilizing: Because the leaves store water much like cacti, the kalanchoe requires soil that drains well, such as a mix of equal parts peat and sand or perlite. During the blooming period, fertilize the soil once every two weeks.

Watering: Because kalanchoes are similar to cacti, they do not like to be watered in excess. Water weekly during the flowering period, but less frequently once the flowers are gone.

Care and propagation: Propagate kalanchoes through seeds and cuttings. The easiest method is through cuttings obtained from offshoots.

Common pests and diseases: Avoid too much water as this will cause root rot. On the contrary, too little water will cause the lower leaves to shrivel and turn yellow. Kalanchoes are relatively disease-free, but keep any eye out for scale, mealybugs, root mealybugs, and mites. Check every so often for caterpillars because they like to eat the leaves.

Other points of interest: Keeping a kalanchoe in continual darkness will enhance flowering. These plants are a commonly distributed around Christmas because that is their peak blooming time.

Orchids

Common name(s): Orchid

Botanical name: *Platanthera spp.*

Plant description: Orchids have become a wildly popular houseplant — and with the amazing variety and color of the flowers, there is an orchid to please any indoor gardener. The orchid species has dozens of cultivars, and some may need special handling, so be sure you know what to expect in terms of care before purchasing one. Generally, orchids have a few fleshy or spike-like leaves and one or more long branches with flowers at the end. Flowers come in all shapes and sizes, but generally they have an intricate shape. Flowers may be a single color or may have stripes, spots, or contrasting eyes. The flowers are unusually long-lasting, and a plant may not bloom again for many months. The new blooms will appear on the same spike, so you can remove the faded flowers, but leave the spike in place.

Light requirements: Orchids grow best in bright, indirect sunlight.

Temperature and humidity: The varieties of orchids have a range of possible growing conditions. Therefore, temperatures for orchids have been grouped into three categories: cool temperature orchids from the *Dendrobium* and *Oncidium* species (60 to 75 degrees), intermediate temperature orchids from the *Paphiopedilum* and *Phalaenopsis* species (65 to 80 degrees), and warm temperature orchids from the *Cattleya* species (70 to 85 degrees). As a tropical plant, most varieties like higher humidity.

Soil and fertilizing: Grow orchids in a rich soil with regular fertilization.

Watering: The watering needs of orchids vary with the origin of the plant. Orchids thrive with frequent watering and occasional misting, but they can be easily damaged with too much water.

Care and propagation: Many orchids are not easy to propagate, but the patient gardener can try to grow new ones from seeds.

Common pests and diseases: Look for mealybugs, slugs, and snails on orchids. Mealybugs are the most serious insect pest for orchids, so wipe the leaves periodically with a damp cloth. Orchids are also susceptible to petal blight and virus infections, which can spread to humans.

Other points of interest: Orchids that adapt well to home and office environments — such as the slipper orchid, the corsage orchid, and the moth orchid — are the ones that were originally forest-dwellers. Many of these original plants have been cultivated into a more easy-to-grow species. Some orchids are fragrant as well.

Peace lily

Common name(s): Peace lily, spath, phyllum, white flag

Botanical name: *Spathiphyllum spp.*

Plant description: Peace lilies, or white flag plants, have dark green, glossy leaves in the shapes of swords growing from graceful curving stems. This plant produces a white flower with a prominent spadix in the center. The peace lily is a graceful specimen with many stems, each producing a dark green, glossy leaf in the shape of a sword. Its name comes from the simple white flowers that sprout from long stems; these flowers have a cowl shape that wraps around a thick flower stem called a spadix. The peace lily's flowers can be removed when they turn green or brown. Peace lilies are versatile plants that can grow large or small and thrive in many types of containers. However, they react strongly to adverse conditions.

Light requirements: This plant prefers medium to low light and will burn if exposed to direct sunlight.

Temperature and humidity: Peace lilies like an average room temperature that ranges between 65 and 75 degrees year-round

Watering: Keep lightly moist all the time and avoid overwatering. Use water this is room temperature.

Soil and fertilizing: If the soil dries out completely, the plant will droop alarmingly, but a good dose of water will perk it up within hours. Fertilize the plant will a full-strength general-purpose treatment twice a month while flowering and every other month when dormant. Peace lilies are also excellent candidates for water culture gardens; the entire plant can be placed in a vase or other container and fertilized every other month.

Care and propagation: The glossy leaves can be kept at their best through occasional misting and wiping with a damp cloth. To propagate this plant, divide the plant by the roots.

Common pests and diseases: These plants are somewhat resistant to many insects and diseases, but keep an eye out for thrips.

Other points of interest: In the right conditions, your peace lily can flower year-round. This plant has excellent ability to remove pollutants from the air.

Seed of Knowledge: In NASA studies, the peace lily was found to help remove chemicals such as formaldehyde, benzene, and carbon monoxide from the air.

Shamrock plant

Common name(s): Shamrock plant, wood sorrel, tropical shamrock

Botanical name: *Oxalis regnellii*

Plant description: Shamrock plants are easy to care for and reward the gardener with profuse stems of white or light pink flowers year-round. The plant gets its name from the triangular leaves that look like clover. The foliage grows on thin stems and has burgundy leaves with green undersides, leaves of deep purple, or leaves in a medium green color.

Light requirements: Situate these plants on a filtered sunny or semi-sunny windowsill. These plants will bloom continuously as long as they receive sufficient light.

Temperature and humidity: Oxalis will grow nicely in an average temperature between 60 and 75 degrees year-round. Protect them from hot or humid conditions as this slows down the production of flowers.

Watering: The plant thrives with light, frequent watering that does not waterlog the plant or allow it to dry out completely.

Soil and fertilizing: Plant them in all-purpose gardening soil mixed with a small amount of peat moss. Fertilize the plants with a full-strength mixture of high phosphorus fertilizer every two weeks.

Care and propagation: Once a year, leach the soil of salt accumulation. Once a flower begins to fade, pinch it off to encourage more flowers. Shamrock plants can be propagated very easily by pulling apart the root crown and replanting the clumps.

Common pests and diseases: Possible pests for the shamrock plant are spider mites, whiteflies, thrips, mealybugs, and scale insects. Be careful not to overwater this plant because it can lead to root rot.

Other points of interest: The shamrock plant is considered one of the easiest houseplants to grow and is the most prolific bloomer.

Zebra plant

Common name(s): Zebra plant, Louisae

Botanical name: *Aphelandra squarrosa*

Plant description: The zebra plant offers two decorative elements: glossy, oval leaves with spectacular white or reddish vein markings, and bright yellow clusters of flower bracts that produce delicate cylindrical flowers. The flowers fade quickly, but the bracts can remain on the plant for a month or two. In the Brazilian rain forest, the zebra plant is an evergreen that grows up to 4 feet tall, but in a windowsill, the plant will grow only 10 to 15 inches tall.

Light requirements: The zebra plant needs direct sun in spring and summer, and medium sunlight in fall, winter, and directly after the flower bracts have died. About three months of intense sunlight after a period of rest will spur the plant to produce a new set of blooms.

Temperature and humidity: This plant grows best in a consistent temperature of 65 to 80 degrees, although cooler temperatures will help the plant through its dormant season. Maintain a moderate to high level of humidity.

Watering: Keep evenly moist, and do not let dry out.

Soil and fertilizing: Pot this plant with a mixture of two parts ordinary potting soil to one part peat moss. The plant develops best in a pot that keeps its roots slightly root-bound. During the production of flowers, fertilize every two weeks with a fertilizer mix containing extra phosphorus; do not fertilize during the dormant fall/winter season.

Care and propagation: Keep the leaves glossy by wiping them occasionally with a damp cloth. Propagate this plant in the spring through stem tip cuttings.

Common pests and diseases: Zebra plants are susceptible to whiteflies and fungus gnats.

Other points of interest: Zebra plants are considered a one-season wonder because it is difficult to get them to re-bloom. However, its striking foliage is enough to make this plant a permanent resident.

Chapter 4

Freshen Up a Room With Fragrant Plants

Fragrant plants are a natural room deodorizer. They are not as treasured now as they were in earlier centuries because of advancements in air purification. Nonetheless, you can still do away with the artificial scents of air fresheners and room deodorizers to enjoy the variety of scented plants and flowers in your home. In fact, some plants produce an aroma so powerful that they can permeate an entire house. And remember, the aromatic chemicals in most of these plants are contained in the flowers, making the fragrance strongest during the flowering period. *Chapter 9 explains the various propagation methods, while Chapter 10 discusses the pests and diseases you might come across in detail.*

> ***Seed of Knowledge:*** *White flowers have the strongest scent. Why? Instead of attracting pollinators by color, white fragrant flowers use a strong, highly volatile scent to attract pollinating insects.*

Carnation

Common name(s): Dianthus, clove pink, carnation, hardy carnation, divine flower, gillyflower

Botanical name: *Caryophyllaceae spp.*

Plant description: A popular flower for cutting, carnation ranges in height from 2 inches to 3 feet. They have a gray-green to bright green stem and leaf and rose-like flowers that come in a variety of colors.

Light requirements: Carnations are happiest in four to five hours of full sun.

Temperature and humidity: Carnations are the most tolerant of humidity than other varieties. However, cool to moderate temperatures produce the best growing climates for this plant.

Watering: Keep soil moist, but avoid overwatering.

Soil and fertilizing: The dianthus prefers a neutral, slightly alkaline, well-drained soil. For continuous blooms, feed every six to eight weeks with an all-purpose liquid fertilizer.

Care and propagation: Remove dead flowers to promote continuous blooming. Carnations can be propagated by seed, cuttings, layering, or division.

Common pests and diseases: Check this plant regularly for aphids, grass-hoppers, and spider mites. Carnations are susceptible to Fusarium wilt, root rot, and crown rot if overwatered.

Other points of interest: Carnations are one of the most common cut flowers used by florists. A native to Eurasia, carnations are mentioned

The flowers of dianthus are edible and frequently used as a garnish in salads; they have a taste similar to nutmeg or clove.

by the classical Greeks and Romans. Dianthus is Greek for "Flower of Zeus."

Easter Lily

Common name(s): Easter lily, Bermuda lily, trumpet lily

Botanical name: *Lilium longiflorum*

Plant description: The Easter lily has become a traditional favorite during the spring season. With two to six trumpet-shaped, white flowers protruding from stems on stalks, Easter lilies are a popular fragrant plant. Depending on the variety, Easter lilies can grow between 12 and 36 inches high and spread 6 to 9 inches wide. The dark, shiny, green foliage on this plant can grow to be 6 inches long and ½-inch wide.

Light requirements: Easter lilies like bright, indirect daylight. Be careful not to expose this plant too long in direct sunlight because the blooms will wilt and fade.

Temperature and humidity: Inside, Easter lilies prefer temperatures between 60 and 65 degrees and can tolerate night temperatures between 55 and 60 degrees. This plant enjoys an average humidity level. However, keep away from drafts, extreme heat, or forced dry air such as heating ducts, fireplaces, or home appliances.

Watering: Water regularly, but do not allow this plant to sit in standing water.

Soil and fertilizing: Easter lilies prefer rich, well-drained soil that is kept moderately moist. They do best with a neutral soil with a 6.5 to 7.0 pH. Potted Easter lilies do not require fertilizer, but if growing from a bulb, apply an all-purpose fertilizer regularly according to its directions.

Care and propagation: Turn your lily every few days to prevent the stems from "leaning" toward the light source. Propagation is usually through bulb offsets or by purchasing parent bulbs.

Common pests and diseases: Look for aphids and spider mites as common pests. Easter lilies are also prone to leaf spots, gray mold, and root rot.

Other points of interest: Easter lilies are native to the Ryukyu Islands of southern Japan. Most of the bulbs purchased in garden centers and nurseries come from a region from Oregon to California known as the "Easter Lily Capital of the World," due to the ideal growing conditions of these regions.

Freesia

Common name(s): Freesia

Botanical name: *Freesia spp.*

Plant description: Freesia flowers are a burst of color along a branch of foliage. The flowers may be single- or double-petaled in colors ranging from pastels to bright yellows and reds. These sweet-smelling branches are excellent cut flowers and bring beauty to a windowsill. Freesias are produced from corms — little bulblets planted about 4 inches below the soil line.

Light requirements: Place the potted corms on a semi-sunny window.

Temperature and humidity: Freesias will thrive in an average room temperature ranging from 65 to 70 degrees.

Watering: Keep the soil evenly moist until flowering is complete.

Soil and fertilizing: Freesias grow best in rich, well-balanced potting soil. The plant will produce flowers within ten weeks of planting, but flowering will slow down if the windowsill temperature rises above 85 degrees.

Care and propagation: Pinch back blooms as they fade in order to encourage more blooms. When the plant stops flowering and the foliage begins to fade, dig up the corms and place them in a paper bag. Store the bag in a place that is cool, dry, and dark. Three to six months later, replant the corms and begin the blooming cycle over again. The plant reproduces by developing new corms. The new, smaller corms may take a year before they are fully productive.

Common pests and diseases: Freesias are not particularly susceptible to any pests or diseases, but make sure you store the corms so that they are not exposed to mold or mildew.

Other points of interest: These fragrant flowers were introduced into cultivation in 1878 and have since been grown for use as cut flowers. Freesia is a popular fragrance for perfumes, scented oils, and bath products.

Gardenia

Common name(s): Gardenia, Cape jasmine

Botanical name: *Gardenia augusta*

Plant description: Gardenias grow large, lovely, creamy-white flowers shaped like many-petaled roses. The flowers and foliage are somewhat waxy, and the leaves are a glossy dark green. The scent of one flower can be so powerful that it perfumes an entire room. In tropical and semi-tropical areas, these plants are outdoor perennials, but many must enjoy their gardenia plants on a windowsill.

Light requirements: Gardenias thrive in bright light or filtered direct sunlight. They need about ten hours of sunlight each day in order to encourage blooming.

Temperature and humidity: Keep gardenias in a normal room temperature between 65 and 70 degrees. Keep plant in a draft-free area to prevent bud loss. High humidity is needed while flower buds are forming. This can be accomplished by placing the plant on a tray of moist pebbles and misting frequently.

Watering: Keep the soil moist but not drenched, and do not allow the pot to sit in water.

Soil and fertilizing: Plant the gardenia in commercial potting soil and fertilize with half-strength acidic fertilizer once a month during the active growing season.

Care and propagation: Once the plant has finished its blooming cycle, pick off the spent flowers and move it to a cool, fairly dark location to rest for a month. Propagate through stem cuttings taken in the spring and early summer. Successful propagation requires root power and high humidity.

Common pests and diseases: Look for spider mites, scale insects, and mealybugs on gardenia plants.

Other points of interest: *Gardenia augusta* was formerly *Gardenia jasminoides*. The name was changed because another plant had already been given the botanical name *Gardenia jasminoides*; this synonym is still incorrectly used, however. Although gardenias can be difficult to grow indoors, it is quite possible given the proper night temperatures.

Hyacinth

Common name(s): Hyacinth, Dutch hyacinth

Botanical name: *Hyacinthus orientalis*

Plant description: The flowers of a hyacinth plant grow on a long, fleshy spike opening to dozens of waxy, star-shaped flowers that emit a powerfully sweet scent. These flowers bloom in shades of yellow, lavender, deep purple, fuchsia, pale pink, and blue. Hyacinths develop from bulbs and are often a symbol of spring, as they usually bloom at that time. However, because they grow from bulbs, they can be forced to bloom in winter or early spring. After blooming, the bulbs can be planted outdoors or kept in a cold, dark storage area until ready to bloom again.

Light requirements: Put the pot in a cool, somewhat dark location until the bulbs begin to produce shoots and then move to a bright, sunny location.

Temperature and humidity: Keep hyacinths in a cool environment from 45 to 60 degrees during the indoor growing period.

Watering: Water thoroughly until the bulb begins to produce shoots. After that, water lightly yet frequently, keeping the soil lightly moist.

Soil and fertilizing: Plant the hyacinth bulbs close together in potting soil mixed with peat, and allow the crowns of the bulbs to peek from the top of the soil.

Care and propagation: After several weeks, the shoots will develop into strap-like leaves about 4 to 6 inches long. The blossoms will open soon afterward and will last between ten days to two weeks. When the forced bulbs stop blooming and the foliage begins to turn brown, cut off the leaves and return the bulbs to a cool, dark, dry location. Alternatively, you can plant the bulbs in a garden.

Common pests and diseases: They are not susceptible to diseases or pests. Make sure that the pot does not become waterlogged, which will cause the bulbs to rot.

Other points of interest: Hyacinths are hardy plants that are tremendously reliable. You can prolong the life of the blooms by moving the plant to the coolest room at night.

Jasmine

Common name(s): Jasmine, Chinese jasmine, winter-blooming jasmine

Botanical name: *Jasminum officinale*

Plant description: The jasmine plant is a flowering vine that originated in tropical Asia. In tropical zones, it can be cultivated as a long-lived perennial. As a houseplant, the vines produce masses of white or pinkish-white flowers shaped into five-point stars. The heady, powerful scent quickly fills the air. The scent of night-blooming jasmine may wake you in the night as the flowers open.

Light requirements: Jasmine plants need at least four hours of direct sunlight each day during the flowering season.

Temperature and humidity: Jasmine plants prefer average temperatures between 65 and 75 degrees and an average humidity level.

Watering: Water the plant when the topsoil feels dry. Keep evenly moist, but water sparingly in the winter.

Soil and fertilizing: It grows best in well-drained soil with a full-strength general fertilizer applied once a month.

Care and propagation: After the flowering season, pick off any remaining flowers and move it to a cool, fairly dark location to rest for a month. Jasmine plants can be propagated from softwood cuttings or by layering low-growing branches.

Common pests and diseases: Mealybugs love jasmine plants; also check for scale insects.

Other points of interest: Because true jasmines are vining plants, train them up a trellis for best results. You can place a small trellis in the pot with your jasmine plant and watch it climb.

Lavender

Common name(s): Lavender

Botanical name: *Lavandula spp.*

Plant description: The lavender plant is an herb that has many uses, from scenting a home, to healing burns and abrasions, to boosting the immune system if ingested. The silvery gray-green leaves produce highly fragrant oil you can experience merely by brushing against the plant. In fact, lavender is grown commercially for use in making perfumes. Lavender plants produce spikes of flowers in several shades of purple, blue, and white. Plants also grow in compact, short varieties, or large, tall cultivars.

Light requirements: Lavender grows best in a sunny location.

Temperature and humidity: Once established, this plant is heat and drought tolerant. Protect lavender from cold temperatures and cold drafts.

Watering: Water the plant when the top third of the soil is dry.

Soil and fertilizing: Plant lavender in sandy soil that drains well. This plant suffers from soil that is too dense and will grow weak and leggy in medium- to low-light conditions.

Care and propagation: To propagate, divide the root sections, and water well before re-planting the divided sections.

Common pests and diseases: Lavender plants do not have any specific pests, because many insects find the plant oil repellent.

Other points of interest: The flower spikes are often dried and used in sachets, potpourri, fragrant bundles, or in making homemade soaps, facial scrubs, and teas. Lavender leaves are sometimes used in cooking, especially in French dishes.

Paperwhites

Common name(s): Paperwhites, daffodil

Botanical name: *Narcissus spp.*

Plant description: Narcissus, also known as paperwhite, is a type of daffodil grown for the creamy white or yellow bell-shaped flowers. Paperwhites have the most powerful fragrance of all daffodils. They grow from bulbs and can be forced to bloom in winter or early spring. After blooming, the bulbs can be planted outdoors or kept in a cold, dark storage area until ready to bloom again.

Light requirements: Once the bulbs begin to produce shoots, move the plant to a bright, sunny location.

Temperature and humidity: During the active growth period, paperwhites will thrive in temperatures that range from 45 to 65 degrees.

Watering: Keep the soil of these paperwhites moderately moist at all times, but not waterlogged.

Soil and fertilizing: Plant the paperwhite bulbs close together in potting soil mixed with peat, and allow the crowns of the bulbs to peek from the top of the soil. Do not fertilize.

Care and propagation: Put the pot in a cool, somewhat dark location until the bulbs begin to produce shoots. After several weeks, the shoots will develop into spikes about 6 to 8 inches tall. The blossoms will open soon afterward and will last a week to ten days. When the forced bulbs stop blooming and the foliage begins to turn brown, cut off the leaves and return the bulbs to a cool, dark, dry location.

Common pests and diseases: Paperwhites are hardy plants that experience little trouble from insects and disease. Make sure the pot does not become waterlogged, which will cause the bulbs to rot.

Other points of interest: To ensure a burst of winter color, plant narcissus bulbs in the fall because it takes about eight to 12 weeks to force bulbs into bloom.

Scented geranium

Common name(s): Scented geranium

Botanical name: *Pelargonium spp.*

Plant description: The common garden geranium has a fragrant cousin, one with pretty leaves that carry unique, varied scents. The leaves secrete oils with smells such as rose, mint, citrus, chocolate, and cinnamon. These fragrant plants also produce geranium flowers in all the usual colors, from white to red to variegated petals. Rose geraniums produce an essential oil used as an ingredient in perfumes, antiseptics, and skin moisturizers.

Light requirements: Like ordinary geraniums, these plants flourish in sunny conditions from a south or west window.

Temperature and humidity: Geraniums like cool to average room temperatures that range from 60 to 75 degrees, with average humidity levels.

Watering: Allow the soil to dry before watering again. Water less in the winter, but do not allow the roots to completely dry out.

Soil and fertilizing: Use a moist, well-draining soil. Commercial potting soil enriched with peat moss will provide the nutrients for this plant.

Care and propagation: In the spring, prune back and repot. Propagate geraniums by taking stem tip cuttings soon after new growth appears. Geraniums can also be grown from seeds.

Common pests and diseases: Geraniums are susceptible to spider mites, whiteflies, aphids, and scale insects and can also develop powdery mildew or anthracnose. Handle these plant problems aggressively. Do not overwater because this causes root rot.

Other points of interest: The fragrance of scented geraniums resides in special cells of the leaves. You can experience the fragrance easily just by touching it — getting a whiff of citrus, mint, chocolate, apple, or even rose. When pruning scented geraniums, keep and dry the leaves to use as a potpourri.

Chapter 5

Spice Up Your Kitchen With Herbal Plants

An herb garden does not have to be strictly utilitarian. The beautiful contrasts of foliage, from broad basil leaves to needle-like rosemary to creeping oregano, can make an interesting statement without further adornment.

Herbs generally have the same nutrient, water, and sun needs as any other plant, though most herbs thrive in as much sunlight as they can receive. Small plant varieties such as oregano, chives, marjoram, parsley, rosemary, and aloe vera work best in the small space of a windowsill garden. In fact, it is always a good idea to keep the healing gel of an aloe vera plant close to your stove for immediate application to any burns or cuts. Unless your window is large, plants with large leaves such as basil, bergamot, mint, and lavender may not receive enough light to truly grow and spread.

*Seed of Knowledge: Herb comes from the Latin word **herba**, which means "grass" or "green crop."*

A Brief History of Herbal Plants

For thousands of years, humans have been using herbal plants to treat illnesses. More than 65 percent of the world's population continues to use herbs today to reap the benefits of their medicinal and culinary properties.

Herbs, when used properly, are safe, reliable, and generally do not create the same side effects as modern-day medications.

The ancient Egyptians were highly skilled with using herbs in their day-to-day lives. The Ebers Papyrus, an ancient medical text from 1500 B.C., references more than 700 herbal remedies that were used by the Egyptians. These ancient Egyptian recipes included herbs such as garlic, aloe, poppy, and caraway.

Chinese culture has practiced using herbs for more than 5,000 years. A Chinese medical encyclopedia called the Shen Nong Ben Cao Jing, which dates back to 2700 B.C., identifies herbal prescriptions for various medical conditions. The herb that is widely associated with the Chinese culture, and is still used today — with popularity — is ginseng. This herb has properties that are said to prolong life with regular use.

It is widely known that Hippocrates (c. 460–377 B.C.) is considered the father of medicine. As far as we can tell, he was the first man to practice medicine and turn it into an art form. He categorized foods and herbs by their properties of being hot, cold, dry, or damp. For example, Hippocrates used warm, dry herbs such as thyme and hyssop to treat chest ailments. Cool, moist plants such as dandelions and violets were used to treat liver disorders. One of Hippocrates' beliefs was that one's strength was in his ability to avoid diseases. Therefore, Hippocrates made ample use of herbs and a strict diet as a basis for treatment of common ailments.

His work was documented extensively in a document titled *De Materia Medica*. This document was developed in A.D. 78 by Pedanius Dioscorides, a Greek physician who worked in Rome. *De Materia Medica* became the standard medical reference for about 1,500 years.

Using the past to heal the present

Aromatherapy and herbs are making a comeback and becoming more popular than ever. Herbalists have made it their business to help people build and maintain optimal health using natural sources such as herbal plants. Today we are finding that because herbs are considered to be food rather than medicine, it seems to be resonating with people that natural is better. Chemically synthesized drugs can produce many unwanted side effects. However, herbs, when take properly and in the right amounts, can help the body cleanse, purify, and heal without substantial side effects. For many, it is making more sense to get back to the basics. According to the World Health Organization, between 65 to 80 percent of the world's population use alternative medicine as their primary healthcare.

The variety of herbs and their ability to treat minor ailments is extensive. From the common cold, sleep disorders, allergies, and weight loss to digestive problems, anxiety disorders, and heart problems, herbal medicines can be effective natural alternatives to chemical or synthetic options. Another important aspect of herbal treatments is that most of the plant can be cultivated including stems, leaves, seeds, barks, and roots. The following are examples of how certain herbs can treat a variety of conditions:

- **Controlling blood sugar** — Well-known herbs such as garlic, cinnamon, cloves, ginkgo biloba, and onion have been shown to control the blood sugar levels associated with diabetes. These herbs have properties that enhance the secretion of insulin, the primary hormone that regulates blood sugar levels.

- **Allergy fighters** — If you suffer from food allergies, insect stings, dust mites, pollen, acne, or eczema, you might benefit from herbs such as nettle, astragalus, ephedra, or butterbur. These herbs are nature's antihistamines, having antioxidant and anti-inflammatory properties.

- **Body detoxification** — Consider the juices of aloe vera, alfalfa, carrots, and garlic if you have problems with digestion. These herbs and herbal remedies have been used to cleanse the colon, assist with food absorption, improve digestion, and boost the immune system.

- **Improving blood circulation** — Herbs such as garlic, ginger, motherwort, hawthorn, and ginkgo biloba are commonly used for problems relating to blood circulation, varicose veins, ulcers, and high blood pressure.

Although there can be a number of benefits to using nature's herbs for maintaining optimum health, always do the necessary research and seek additional help before using any of these herbs. Many have side effects just like medications — you may be allergic to herbs; there are contraindications of using herbs with other herbs or medicines; and there are herbs that should be avoided with certain pre-existing conditions, such as pregnancy.

CASE STUDY: SLOWING DOWN AND RECONNECTING WITH NATURE

Karen Creel, Gardin Chick
Chickamuaga, Georgia
www.gardenchick.com

I have always liked bringing a little bit of the outdoors inside, especially in the winter, so windowsill gardening seemed like a good fit. Windowsill gardening has always been a hobby for me, and much of it has been through trial and error. Now that I run a business creating products from the garden, herb plants are my favorite. I prepare herb seasonings, dream pillows, bath and body products, and gardening decor.

Flowering Plants

Bergamot

Amaryllis

Anthurium

Begonias

Bush Lily

Gardenia

Lavender

Orchid

Freesia

Jasmine

Cyclamen

African Violet

Hibiscus

Double-Flowering
Begonia

All photographs on this page are provided by Angela Williams Duea

Scarlet Star Bromeliad

All photographs on this page are provided by Angela Williams Duea

Purple Variegated Wandering Jew

All photographs on this page are provided by Angela Williams Duea

Nonflowering Plants

Croton

Dumbcane

All photographs on this page are provided by Angela Williams Duea

Blood Leaf

Haworthia Succulent

All photographs on this page are provided by Angela Williams Duea

Golden Star Cactus

Golden Barrel Cactus

Ball Cactus

All photographs on this page are provided by Angela Williams Duea

Pothos

All photographs on this page are provided by Angela Williams Duea

Rabbit's Foot Fern

Snake Plant and
Boston Fern

Variegated Polypody Fern

All photographs on this page are provided by Angela Williams Duea

English Ivy

Spider Plant

Umbrella Tree

All photographs on this page are provided by Angela Williams Duea

Arrowhead Plant

Echeveria Succulent

All photographs on this page are provided by Angela Williams Duea

Flowering Coleus

Because many of the herbs I use for my recipes come from the Mediterranean and North Africa regions, they require six or more hours of sun daily and a well-drained location. Planting an herbal window garden provides fresh herbs right at my fingertips.

I have three primary garden themes for which I grow herbs. These gardens are:

1. Apothecary
2. Insect repellent
3. Scent gardens

For these themed herb gardens, I cultivate herbs such as lavender, thyme, calendula, catnip, yarrow, chamomile, tansy, chives, mints, bee balm, cone plant, rosemary, and St. John's wort.

I maintain my plants by first placing them in the proper light requirements. All of my plants require watering when dry to touch, so I do not overwater, and I turn them frequently. In the winter, I do not feed my plants with extra fertilizer, but in the spring, I start with a basic houseplant fertilizer and fertilize per directions all summer.

Herbs generally do not have many pests, due their natural repellent properties. To minimize the spread of any pests that try to inhabit my plants, I space my plants a fair distance apart, I do not overwater them, and I check them often. I usually pick off any bugs I find and dispose of them. Also, I do not water in the evening when the plants will be wet all night. If I do have to use anything to mitigate pests or disease, I use a natural insecticidal soap.

Thirteen Great Herbs for Your Windowsill

Before selecting the herbs to grow on your windowsill, you may want to create several different gardens for specific uses. For example, consider these special arrangements:

- For a culinary herb garden to provide seasonings for meals, try growing basil, chives, cilantro, dill, marjoram, mint, oregano, and rosemary.

- For a medicinal herb garden for homeopathic healing, try growing chamomile, bergamot, aloe vera, lavender, catnip, comfrey, parsley, and St. John's wort.

- For a cosmetic herb garden for natural lotions, bath oils, perfumes, and astringents, try growing lavender, feverfew, lemon balm, lemon verbena, and chamomile.

- For a tea garden for making natural, organic beverages, try growing mint, chamomile, lemon balm, lemon verbena, tarragon, anise, and cardamom.

- For a fragrance garden for making potpourri, sachets, nosegays, and wreaths, try growing mint, lavender, basil, angelica, lemon balm, rosemary, sage, and myrtle.

Even if you do not intend to use herbs for medicinal or culinary purposes, many of the following herbs have foliage that provides fragrance and decorative form to your garden. You will find that most of these herbs also have pollen-producing flowers that attract butterflies, bees, and hummingbirds. They may not be able to get through the window to actually land on your plants, but you may see a visitor or two trying to get a "taste" of your windowsill herb garden.

Basil

Common name(s): Basil, sweet basil, spicy globe basil

Botanical name: *Ocimum basilicum*

Plant description: This familiar and most popular plant is cultivated as a culinary herb, condiment, and spice. Known for its sweet fragrant leaves, basil adds a licorice-like flavor to salads, tomato-based dishes, and pesto sauces. A native of tropical Asia, this low-growing plant has pointed, oval leaves that sit on opposing branches in a flat plane. There are many cultivars of basil, but the most common is *Ocimum basilicum*, or sweet basil. The basil plant contains and essential oil that can be cultivated for use in foods or fragrances. The most popular use of the basil plant comes from the leaves. Pinch a handful of leaves directly off the basil plant to add to salads. When basil leaves are cut and dried, they work well as a spice.

Light requirements: Basil can be grown successfully indoors by a bright window that provides full sun.

Temperature and humidity: Basil plants thrive in warm conditions.

Watering: Water basil plants regularly. Be sure to allow for the water to completely drain before watering again.

Soil and fertilizing: Plant basil in a humus-rich, moist, and well-drained soil.

Care and propagation: Pinch the tips of the basil plant regularly to encourage bushiness and vigorous growth. Basil is easy to grow from seed.

Common pests and diseases: Basil is usually not susceptible to any pests because of the strong smell of its leaves.

Other points of interest: Basil is a great companion plant to tomatoes because they both like warm, moist growing conditions. They also make a good pair in a salad. Basil is most flavorful during July to mid-August. Basil is easy to care for and fast-growing.

Chamomile

Common name(s): Chamomile, Roman chamomile

Botanical name: *Chamaemelum nobile*

Plant description: When you need to slow down a bit or just need something to calm your nerves, having easy access to your chamomile plant my just be the answer. Because of its apple-like fragrance and flavor, chamomile is a popular herb for herbal teas. Cultivated as an herb for its calming and sedative properties, chamomile has also been used in bath products, hair rinses, and cosmetics. This attractive plant is a great addition to any herb garden. White, daisy-like flowers with yellow centers appear in the summer.

Light requirements: Chamomile prefers to grow in locations with full sun.

Temperature and humidity: This plant grows best in moderate temperatures between 65 to 75 degrees. It can tolerate temperatures up to 85 degrees but will decline in hot temperatures. Chamomile prefers moderate to low humidity levels; high humidity will cause fungal problems.

Watering: Chamomile plants need moderate water.

Soil and fertilizing: Chamomile thrives in a moist, rich soil.

Care and propagation: Cut back regularly to encourage dense, bushy growth. Chamomile is easily propagated from seeds. You can also propagate chamomile by division in early spring or fall or by cutting the basal shoots.

Common pest and diseases: Chamomile is susceptible to aphids, mealybugs, and powdery mildew.

Other points of interest: Harvest the flowers of chamomile when they are in full bloom. They can be used to make chamomile tea, which is known for its calming, sedative nature. Be careful with the foliage of the chamomile plant; it may aggravate skin allergies.

Chives

Common name(s): Chives

Botanical name: *Allium schoenoprasum*

Plant description: As the smallest species of the onion family, chives are a clump-forming plant that grows between 12 and 19 inches tall. Chives produce pale purple clusters of flowers on a leafless stem that sits atop a clump of foliage. These onions are most popular as an addition to bake potatoes, but they also work well in dips and sprinkled on salads.

Light requirements: Chives grow best in full sun.

Temperature and humidity: Chives require moderate temperatures and humidity.

Watering: Because chives are fairly shallow-rooted, water frequently.

Soil and fertilizing: Although chives grow best in well-drained, rich soil that is enhanced with organic matter with a 6.0 to 7.0 pH, they can tolerate moist soils and a low nutrient requirement.

Care and propagation: Chives are easy to start from seed with a soil temperature above 65 degrees before germination.

Common pests and diseases: Onion maggots are a primary problem for chives.

Other points of interest: Once established, chives require little attention. Chives have been said to increase appetite and easy digestion. Once dried, chives do not keep their flavor.

Cilantro/Coriander

Common name(s): Cilantro, coriander

Botanical name: *Coriandrum sativum*

Plant description: This plant serves a dual purpose. The feather green leaves of the *coriandrum* plant are cultivated as cilantro, while the seeds are used as a main ingredient in curry powder. Coriander can grow to a height of 2 feet with a 9-inch spread. This plant produces flowers in late summer that are small, white, and form in clusters.

Light requirements: Full sun or partial shade is best for growing coriander.

Temperature and humidity: Coriander does not grow well in humid conditions. It needs a dry, warm environment.

Watering: Keep the soil of the coriander plant evenly moist.

Soil and fertilizing: Use a humus-rich, well-drained soil for coriander.

Care and propagation: The stems of coriander are weak and may need help from a stake. Harvest the leaves as needed, and gather the seeds just as the tops start to wither. Coriander is best propagated by seed after danger of frost has passed.

Common pests and diseases: There are no pests that are especially problematic for coriander, but it can be susceptible to fungal diseases if overwatered.

Other points of interest: A common spice used on Greek and Asian cooking, coriander has a sweet taste that is often compared to that of an orange peel. Its leaves, called cilantro, are popular in Mexican and Asian cuisine. This plant is often used to treat digestive problems and colic.

Dill

Common name(s): Dill

Botanical name: *Anethum graveolens*

Plant description: Dill has made a name for itself as it has shown up in historical records as a culinary and medicinal herb. Dill plants can grow to be 3 feet tall and spread 8 inches or more. The plant displays feathery foliage and clusters of yellow flowers blooming at the tops of sturdy stems.

Light requirements: Like most herbs, dill likes full sun but will tolerate some afternoon shade.

Temperature and humidity: Dill plants like cool weather.

Watering: Keep the soil of dill plants evenly moist.

Soil and fertilizing: Plant dill in a moist, well-drained soil.

Care and propagation: Use a deep container for dill plants because they often have the long roots. Your dill plant may require staking. Propagate dill by sowing seeds. Dill may self-sow in subsequent years.

Common pests and diseases: Dill attracts predatory insects, butterflies, and caterpillars, which are particularly fond of dill.

Other points of interest: Dill is one of the easiest herbs to grow and is a perfect choice for beginners. It is often used to treat colic or gas in children. Do not grow dill near fennel because they will cross-pollinate.

Marjoram

Common name(s): Marjoram, sweet marjoram

Botanical name: *Origanum majorana*

Plant description: A close relative of oregano, sweet marjoram has a milder flavor and fragrance. It is an upright plant that has light green, hairy leaves. In the summer, it produces white or pink flowers. This plant can grow to be 2 feet tall and spread to a width of 8 inches.

Light requirements: Marjoram grows best in full sun.

Temperature and humidity: Marjoram is a frost-sensitive perennial. It can grow in warm climates as a perennial and cooler climates as an annual.

Watering: Marjoram plants prefer soil that is kept evenly moist.

Soil and fertilizing: Marjoram has no particular preference for soil as long as it is well-drained.

Care and propagation: To keep marjoram plants looking neat, cut out all the dead wood, and remove dead flowers and stalks. Propagate marjoram easily by seed or from summer cuttings. Roots may be divided in the fall.

Common pests and diseases: Marjoram is susceptible to root rot and fungal diseases if overwatered.

Other points of interest: Marjoram is primarily a culinary herb, but it also has medicinal value. It has been used as a general tonic to treat digestive and respiratory system disorders.

Mint

Common name(s): Mint

Botanical name: *Mentha spp.*

Plant description: Grown for centuries as a food additive, rubbing aid, and medicine, the mint plant grows wild in Southern and Central Europe. Mint is cultivated primarily for its menthol production for commercial use. Peppermint is the strong scent of the mint family, and it is widely used in candies, toothpaste, mouthwashes, and medications. The most difficult thing about mint plants is choosing which ones of the 600 varieties to grow. These include spearmint, apple mint, licorice mint, chocolate mint, basil mint, and orange mint — to name a few.

Light requirements: Mint plants prefer a full sun environment with intermittent shade conditions.

Temperature and humidity: Keep the temperature cool to average, from 55 to 70 degrees; humidity should be moderate.

Watering: Keep the soil of mint plants evenly moist.

Soil and fertilizing: The soil of a mint plant should be humus-rich and slightly moist.

Care and propagation: Harvest young leaves as needed and use them fresh from the plant or dry the leaves to use for later. Mint plants are easy to grow as a windowsill plant. The mint plant can be invasive because once it goes to seed, it spreads easily. Grow these plants in a pot without a bottom. This will help to control spreading because the roots are contained inside the walls of the pot.

Common pests and diseases: Mint is usually not susceptible to any pests because of the strong smell of its leaves. However, leaf rust may be a problem.

Other points of interest: Mint is a medicinal wonder used as an essential oil to treat indigestion, headaches, colic, and irritable bowel syndrome. Another common use for mint leaves is in herbal teas.

Oregano

Common name(s): Oregano, Greek oregano

Botanical name: *Origanum vulgare*

Plant description: A close relative of marjoram, oregano has deep, bold aroma that adds flavor to well-known dishes such as spaghetti and pizza. This plant is grown abundantly in Great Britain, Italy, Mexico, and parts of South America. Oregano leaves vary among the different cultivars, but mainly they are on square stems, and are small, oval, opposite, toothed or smooth edges. The leaves range in size from ½ inch to 2 inches long.

Light requirements: Oregano thrives in sun or partial shade.

Temperature and humidity: This herb does well in temperatures between 60 to 75 degrees and average humidity.

Watering: Keep a routine watering regiment for the oregano plant.

Soil and fertilizing: Oregano is not picky about the soil as long as it is well-drained and porous.

Care and propagation: Oregano can be propagated easily by seed. Once planted, it spreads quickly by underground runners. It can also be divided and then replanted.

Common pests and diseases: Check oregano periodically for spider mites and aphids. If the soil is not well-drained, it can lead to root rot.

Other points of interest: The Greeks often used oregano to stop convulsions. It was also used to counteract being poisoned by opium and hemlock. In Greek, *oros* means "mountain" and *ganos* means "joy;" therefore, one could translate oregano as "joy of the mountains." Today, oregano is often used medicinally as an expectorant and to aid in digestion.

Sage

Common name(s): Sage, Holt's mammoth, Berggarten, tricolor

Botanical name: *Salvia officinalis*

Plant description: A woody evergreen, sage grows as a mounding plant with soft, gray-green leaves. Similar to the mint family, *salvia* leaves are directly opposite each other on a four-sided stem. Sage produces pink, white, and lavender flowers in late spring. The flowers grow in clusters along a spiky stem. The plant itself can grow anywhere from 6 to 24 inches high, and it can spread to a width of 24 inches. More than 900 species of *salvia* exist, including shrubs, herbs, perennials, and annuals.

Light requirements: Sage prefers a sunny location but can tolerate light shade.

Temperature and humidity: This plant grows best in warm environments.

Watering: Keep the soil evenly moist until established. After that, sage plants are drought tolerant.

Soil and fertilizing: Average alkaline soil is good for sage, as long as it is well drained.

Care and propagation: Keep sage plants well-pruned to encourage young shoots with a strong flavor. Consistent, routine pruning also prevents the plant from becoming leggy. Propagate sage from summer cuttings. Seeds are unreliable and slow to flower.

Common pests and diseases: Check your sage plant periodically for spider mites. Wilt and root rot can also become a problem if the plant is overwatered.

Other points of interest: Sage is known for its unique flavoring in turkey stuffing and Italian sausage. Sage has antiseptic properties and is often used as a gargle for sore throats.

Rosemary

Common name(s): Rosemary

Botanical name: *Rosmarinus offici-nalis*

Plant description: Grown as a perennial evergreen shrub, rosemary will grow to a height between 3 and 5 feet. It is an attractive shrub with pine needle-like leaves and bluish flowers that last through spring and summer.

Light requirements: Grow rosemary in a location that is protected from wind and rain, allowing the plant exposure to plenty of sun. A southern windowsill would be ideal for this.

Temperature and humidity: Rosemary can survive up to 30 years in a warm location. However, in hot weather, this plant enjoys a good soaking.

Watering: Keep the soil evenly moist.

Soil and fertilizing: Plant rosemary in a deep, sandy, well-drained soil.

Care and propagation: Be sure to plant rosemary in a large enough pot to hold its extensive root system. Keep the size in check by clipping the thick shrub. Rosemary can be propagated in early summer from cuttings of the twisted wood of non-flowering branches. It can also be grown easily from seed.

Common pests and diseases: Scale insects and mealybugs can pose a problem for rosemary plants.

Other points of interest: Scientists and psychology professors Joel Warm

> *Seed of Knowledge: Rosemary is a commonly used in potpourris, cosmetics, shampoos, and disinfectants."*

and Dr. William Dember of the University of Cincinnati conducted an extensive study in the 1990s. The study was performed on university students who were asked to inhale the fragrance of the rosemary plant. From this study, they discovered that the aroma of the rosemary plant stimulates the memory.

Parsley

Common name(s): Parsley, curled parsley

Botanical name: *Petroselinum crispum*

Plant description: Parsley is a clump-forming biennial that grows to about 12 inches tall and 24 inches wide. This particular cultivar has curly, bright green leaves. The leaflets are finely divided on long stems, and the plant has a rounded shape like that of a mound. In its second summer, parsley grows stalks with small yellow flowers. Parsley is a native of southern Europe and the eastern Mediterranean regions, but today it is cultivated all around the world for its leaves, seeds, and roots.

Light requirements: Parsley grows well in full sun or partial shade.

Temperature and humidity: Parsley performs best at temperatures ranging between 50 and 70 degrees. It will suffer in hot and humid environments when temperatures reach more than 90 degrees.

Watering: Keep the soil moist but not overly wet.

Soil and fertilizing: Parsley prefers a humus-rich, moist, and well-drained soil.

Care and propagation: Harvest regularly throughout the summer to keep the plant producing. Parsley plants need to be regularly pruned to enable new leaves to mature. Start parsley where you intend to grow it because this plant does not transplant well. Instead, start either with a well-rooted seedling or directly sow from seed.

Common pests and diseases: Caterpillars are a common resident of the parsley plant.

Other points of interest: Often used as a garnish, parsley is rich in vitamins and minerals. It is a good source of vitamin C, folic acid, and iron. It is commonly used as a breath freshener after eating garlic- or onion-rich foods. Parsley has also been known to treat gout, rheumatism, and arthritis.

Tarragon

Common   name(s):   Tarragon, French tarragon

Botanical name: *Artemisia dracunculus*

Plant description: Tarragon is an aromatic herb that is used extensively in the kitchen as a flavor enhancement to sauces, soups, fish, poultry, and vegetables. It is a sun-loving perennial that is native to southern Europe. Mature tarragon plants can grow to be 36 inches high with dark, shiny green leaves. These leaves cover the stem from the base of the plant to the top of the stem.

Light requirement: Although they can survive in partial shade, tarragon plants prefer six hours of full sunlight to grow properly.

Temperature and humidity: Tarragon does not do well in environments that are cold and harsh.

Watering: Do not overwater.

Soil and fertilizing: Tarragon prefers a soil that is rich, sandy, well-drained, and limed. Fertilize once when establishing plants; no more is needed after that.

Care and propagation: Handle tarragon plants carefully because they are prone to bruising. Harvest the leaves in midsummer, and use the leaves fresh or frozen. Picking the leaves in the early morning is said to capture the best flavor. Propagate tarragon from division or stem cuttings rather than from seed.

Common pests and diseases: There are no known pests that post any threat to tarragon plants. Rather, tarragon is often kept as a companion plant to repel pests from other plants in the garden. Root rot and mildew may be a problem if soil becomes waterlogged.

Other points of interest: The leaves of the tarragon plant have become an essential ingredient in the French cuisine.

Thyme

Common name(s): Thyme

Botanical name: *Thymus vulgaris*

Plant description: A native of the Mediterranean and southern Italy, thyme is a semi-woody shrub with ½-inch long gray-green leaves. Thyme grows in a bushy fashion, reaching up to 12 inches in height and up to 24 inches in width. In the summer, it produces pale pink flowers at the tips of the stems.

Light requirements: Thyme likes full sun, but it will tolerate partial shade.

Temperature and humidity: This herb does well with average temperatures and humidity.

Watering: Thyme requires regular watering.

Soil and fertilizing: Thyme performs best in neutral to alkaline, or basic, soils.

Care and propagation: Thyme does well in a pot that allows it to cascade over the side. Once established, the only care needed for this plant is regular pruning to remove dead flowers and old wood. Thyme can be grown from seed, but it can also be propagated from stem cuttings and division.

Common pests and diseases: In southern regions, thyme is prone to disease and insect infestation.

Other points of interest: Thyme is used in the kitchen to spice up fish, poultry, soups, and vegetables. Medicinally, thyme and thyme oil have been used as disinfectants, antiseptics, and mouthwashes. Thyme oil, thymol, is active in fighting salmonella and staphylococcus bacteria.

Chapter 6

Creating the Optimal Growing Environment

When I spent time in Puerto Rico and other islands in the Caribbean, I was surprised to see gigantic versions of my houseplants growing along roads and in gardens. Tree-sized hibiscus, dumbcane, and fuchsia flowers were all around. It was then I learned that many of the plants we bring indoors as houseplants are actually bred in tropical climates. It makes sense; a home has a climate similar to tropical environments: moderate warmth and moisture, light levels similar to the levels found under a tropical forest canopy, and freedom from vast fluctuations in temperature.

However, each home has its own climate, and within each home, there are "microclimates" that are a big factor in determining whether or not your windowsill plants will thrive. The amount of sunlight, artificial light, air quality, exposure to drafts or heating ducts, and humidity level should all be considered when choosing a plant. Your plants rely on you to set up an environment in which they can flourish because they cannot simply pull up their roots and migrate to a better climate. When you do not meet your plants' needs, you will eventually cause them to become sickly and die. On the other hand, if you provide them with optimal growing conditions, you will be rewarded with bountiful growth for years to come.

Shedding Some Light On the Subject

Light is one of the most important factors in a plant's health. Without the right lighting conditions, a plant cannot produce food through photosynthesis. Too much light can burn plants, and too little light will leave them unable to thrive and grow. Many plants come with a label that indicates what kind of light they need. Sunny plants need several hours of direct light on their foliage. Semi-sunny plants require some direct contact with light during the day. Semi-shade plants will prosper in a window that provides indirect light that does not necessarily touch the plants, while shade plants can do well in darker places if the amount of light is still enough to read a book.

Let the sun shine in

Assess, select, and plan your site carefully. Whether you have only one window for setting up a windowsill garden or several windows or rooms to choose from, think about the amount of sunlight that will come in the window throughout the year. In the Northern Hemisphere, north-facing windows let in the least amount of light and are suitable for semi-shade or shade-loving plants. South-facing windows will give plants the most hours of direct sunlight each day, which is best for plants that need sunny or partially sunny conditions to grow well. Eastern windows provide bright sunlight in the mornings but rarely produce as much heat as west-facing windows do in the afternoons. Each of these windows is suitable for sun-loving plants.

However, your house's particular lighting conditions are bound to vary. You might not be situated on a strict north/south or east/west line, or you might have roof overhangs, trees, or bushes outside that block the sunlight coming inside. Even dirty windows or dark screens will change the quality of light. Factor this into the amount of light your windowsill plants will absorb. You should also consider seasonal changes in lighting conditions. In northern latitudes, there are longer hours of daylight in the spring and summer, and there are shorter hours of sunlight in the fall and winter. The angle of the sun in the winter makes the light during these months less intense, and overcast days reduce the average amount of sunlight on your plants. By contrast, plants that receive proper amounts of light during the winter will be scorched in the summer when the light is much more intense.

Some plants are sensitive to the actual number of hours of light they receive, especially some of the flowering plants. While most plants can grow and bloom regardless of the length of the day or the amount of daylight, some plants need a series of long days before they will begin to bloom. These long-day plants include many annuals, such as chrysanthemums or herbs — plants that would benefit from long summer days in an outdoor environment as well as indoors in front of a sunny window. You can coax these plants to bloom during shorter days by extending their "days" to 14 hours or more with artificial light.

Short-day plants — such as begonias, Christmas cacti, and kalanchoes — need long, dark nights of 12 hours or more before they will begin to bloom. They are plants that bloom in fall or winter in their natural habitats, when the days begin to shorten and nights are longer. Coaxing plants to bloom can be a little more difficult for an indoor gardener because your plants are located in rooms where you will be turning lights on at night. You can help these plants to bloom by covering them with a box or opaque paper bag after 12 hours of daylight, or you can move them to a closet at twilight each night and return them to their spots during the day. Once you see flower buds beginning to form, you can leave them in their customary spots and enjoy the blooms.

Go artificial for poor lighting conditions

All plants need light, but they do not necessarily need natural light. Plants can thrive under incandescent and fluorescent lighting, especially as a supplement to sunlight. However, a windowsill plant will receive some amount of natural light each day and will only benefit from additional light.

In most houses, you will likely be using the room where your windowsill plant is located, and the plant will get an extra boost of light each night from your room's lighting. If this light is not enough for your plants, you can install a spotlight or additional light fixture over the plant, or add wattage to your light fixtures. Be sure that any artificial light sources are more than 12 inches from the plant.

Ordinary incandescent lights are less helpful to plants because their light is on the red side of the spectrum, and plants need a balance between red and blue rays. Fluorescent lights provide a better balance. There are also special plant light bulbs designed to provide the proper light balance, but experts are mixed in their opinions of these.

What your plant is telling you about the light

One of the most important skills you can pick up as a gardener is the knack for reading your plant's signals. If you have a pet, you can likely understand what the animal is communicating even though it does not speak your language. Likewise, you can read a baby's body language, posture, and expressions. Plants can also communicate about their health through easy-to-read signs, once you learn to recognize them.

When your plant does not receive enough light, the plant will display a combination of the following signs:

- Foliage more pale than normal

- Plant bending in the direction of the light source
- Root or stem rot
- Susceptibility to disease or pests
- Weak, elongated growth with few leaves
- Abnormally small leaves with thin, floppy texture
- Slow growth or no growth at all
- No blooms or poor flowering
- Significant, continuous leaf loss

Plants that continue to suffer from lack of light will eventually die. To rescue these plants, you can add another light source to the area, such as a clip-on lamp or a new overhead light fixture. If the light fixtures in the area are already sufficient, try leaving the lights on for several extra hours each day to give your plants more exposure to the light, even if you are not using the room. If these changes do not help the condition of your plant, and you do not see signs of improvement within three to four weeks, you will need to choose a new site for your plant.

Most plants will bend toward the source of sunlight, unless they are already receiving too much light. Eventually your plant could grow in a horizontal stem or risk tipping over. Once you have corrected the amount of light, even the growth and help the plant to grow straight by giving it a quarter-turn in the same direction each time you water it.

If you move a plant too quickly from a sunny area to a darker one, it can lose many of its leaves due to shock. Those leaves were acclimated to an environment in which much photosynthesis was happening, and the plant will shed the leaves it no longer needs. However, the shock is dangerous to the plant; it is better to make the change slowly over several weeks. Move the plant to the new location for a few hours each day, and slowly increase the time it spends there. The plant will go through a period of adjustment, but if all other factors are optimal, it will adapt.

When your plant is absorbing too much light, it will display several of the following signs:

- Abnormally compact, bunched growth
- Wilted or downward-curling leaves
- Leaves with a darker color and thicker texture than normal leaves
- Brown burn marks or pale, translucent spots where the light has contacted the foliage
- Yellow, thickened stems
- Plant's soil dries quickly
- Plant is susceptible to pests and disease

Some plants exposed to too much light will not die, but they will have difficulty thriving. Others will burn so badly that they can never recover. To protect the plant and prevent further damage, move the plant away from the window and reduce the amount of artificial light it receives. It is also possible the plant is getting sufficient sunlight but is overheated by the temperature change of the sunny window. If you touch the leaves of the plant during midday, you should be able to feel whether the leaves are being "broiled" by the sun. Even moving the plant a few inches away from the window can take care of the problem.

You can also put up sheer curtains as a filter to correct the lighting conditions. You might not even need to shield the plant all day — perhaps it only needs protection during the most intense sunlight hours. In addition, if there is room on your windowsill, you can put the light-sensitive plant behind other plants that can tolerate higher concentrations of light.

It is especially important to protect plants you move from low-light to bright-light conditions, just as you would protect your skin when you are outside for significant periods of time. A leaf's surface can be "sunburned" like your skin when it is not exposed to sun in increments, and it needs to build up protection in the same way suntan lotion protects you from burning. Gradually increase the number of hours the plant spends in the brighter location while avoiding the hottest and most intense periods of sunlight for the first few weeks.

Watering Basics for Your Windowsill Plants

The right amount of water is crucial to your plant's health. The plant's roots absorb the water, and the stems pipe the water up to the foliage and flowers, bringing nutrients to the surface to help produce energy. Plants respire as we do, breathing out oxygen; they also perspire by letting some of the water evaporate from the foliage.

In nature, most plants receive water through rain, which also washes the leaves while draining down into the soil. At home, we water plants at the soil level, but most plants benefit from having their leaves misted. Plants enjoy an occasional shower in the bathtub or a spraying in the sink. If you do this, be sure to let the water evaporate before placing the plant in direct sun — the water beads will act as magnifying glasses to burn the leaves. A plant such as an African violet should never have wet leaves, because this causes the leaves to rot.

A watering can or pitcher, especially one with a long spout for reaching high places, will help you water your plants. Pour the water into the soil at even intervals around the surface of the pot, and keep pouring until you see water draining out into the saucer. Wait about an hour, and then pour off any water still in the saucer so that it does not encourage mold or rot in the roots. After you water a plant a few times, you will start to notice how long it takes before the plant dries out and needs more water.

How much is too much...or too little?

Your houseplants depend on you to provide the right amount of water for their health. If the plant receives too much water, the standing water will rot the root system and cause the circulation system to break down. Too little water will stop the flow of nutrients, and the leaves will begin to die back. However, with a little knowledge, some practice, and attention to your plant's signs, you will easily be able to give the plant all it needs.

Plants have different watering requirements, and these are often indicated on the label when you purchase them. If not, ask the seller for information. Most cacti and succulents need little water and humidity, because in their natural environments they receive rain only rarely; these plants are designed to store water against drought. Many houseplants go into a resting or dormant stage throughout the winter, triggered by short, cool days and a lack of sunlight or artificial light. During this season, water less often, and if the plant needs the dormant season to produce blooms, make sure they are not exposed to much artificial light.

Plants also have moist, moderate, or dry soil needs. "Moist" means that the soil must never be allowed to dry out before watering again — but the plant should not stand in water. "Moderate" means that the surface of the soil can dry out before watering again. "Dry" plants should be watered only when about two-thirds of the soil is completely dry.

Rather than investing in expensive and unpredictable digital moisture meters, use the "touch test" to determine when your plants need more water. Press a finger into the surface of the soil to determine when to water moist and moderate plants. Insert a toothpick or chopstick into the soil of dry plants to determine how far down the moisture has receded. If the soil is dry, it will not cling to the toothpick or chopstick. Moderately moist soil will have a small amount of soil that clings to the wood. Damp soil will cling to the surface of the wood when you pull it out. Once you know your plants' basic requirements, you can adjust them to your individual conditions.

Water more often if:
- Your plant has many tiny roots that you can see at its base
- Your plant produces big leaves
- Your plant is in a porous pot such as clay, which allows quicker evaporation than plastic pots
- Your plant is much larger than its pot
- Your soil contains a large amount of peat, sand, or other light planting media (*see Chapter 7 for further information*)
- Your pot is in a warm, sunny location
- Your household humidity is low

Water less often if:
- Your plant has thick, fleshy leaves
- Your plant is smaller than the pot
- Your plant is in an indirect-sun or low-light location
- Your plant's soil is thick or full of clay
- Your plant is in a location with high humidity, such as a bathroom
- Your plant's pot does not have any drainage holes

Water types for optimal growth

When you water your plants, you should always use water at room temperature, especially if you are watering tropical plants. Plants absorb water best if they are watered in the morning; this also prevents any water droplets on the leaves from burning the plants in morning's colder light.

Plants can do well with water straight from the tap. However, plants such as the cast iron plant, the spider plant, and the entire *Dracaena* species can be damaged by city water fortified with fluoride or purified with chlorine. You will notice the leaf tips and edges start to brown in these sensitive plants. If this happens, let the water sit overnight to allow the chemicals to dissipate before using the water for your plants.

If you have sensitive plants or low-quality water, you have the following options:

- Collect water from outdoor taps often not connected to the water softener.

- Save rainwater from the downspout of the rain gutter to water your plants.

- Buy bottled water or use water that has run through a water purifier.

- If you have a freshwater aquarium, you can use that water to irrigate your plants — the water has already been corrected for the health of your fish, and the nutrients in the fishbowl will benefit your plants.

Keeping humidity levels optimal

Humidity is an assessment of the amount of water evaporated in the air. When measuring the amount of water vapor in the air, we measure the relative humidity — the amount of water vapor in the air at a given temperature, compared to the amount of water vapor the air can possibly hold at that temperature. When the air is holding all the water vapor it can hold at that temperature, it is at 100 percent relative humidity. At this level, called the dew point, water will begin to condense. Inside your home, you will see this condensation on windows and mirrors first when the warmer, wetter air contacts a cold pane of glass.

Interestingly, the amount of humidity also changes our perception of the temperature. Hot weather feels even hotter when it is humid; cold air feels even colder with a low relative humidity. During a cold winter, you can increase your warmth without turning up the heat by adding more humidity to your home. Humans are most comfortable in an environment of relative humidity between 30 and 60 percent. A desert environment has an average relative humidity of 25 percent, but in our homes, an average relative humidity of 35 to 40 percent is ideal.

Most plants, excluding cacti, thrive on humidity. Humidity is good for your health as well. Winter can be especially dry. You notice the change because of dry eyes and nasal passages, flaky skin, and irritating static electricity; dry coughs, sneezing, and susceptibility to colds are also a sign of extreme dryness. Plants are sensitive to the change in humidity and will require more frequent watering, but they could also benefit from increased humidity. To help your own health and the health of your plants, use a few of the following techniques to add more moisture to the air in your home:

- When doing laundry, take clothes and towels out of the laundry before they are completely dry. Hang the semi-dry clothes on hangers, and drape towels over chairs or on a laundry rack. As they dry, the moisture will evaporate into the room and return moisture to the air.

- When washing dishes by hand, allow the dishes to air-dry. When using a dishwasher, skip the drying phase. Open the door and allow the steam to escape and the dishes to dry naturally.

- If you mist your plants, mist your curtains at the same time — but test for water-fastness first. The mist will return to the air and change the humidity.

- Put a layer of small pebbles on each flowerpot tray. Cover the pebbles with water, and replenish as the water evaporates.

- Place a bowl or cup of water on windowsills or near heating vents. The water will evaporate slowly into the air, pushed by air currents.

- Skip the bathroom fan when you take a shower. Instead, open the bathroom doors afterwards, and let the steam escape into the house.

- Use a kettle rather than the microwave to heat water for your tea or other hot beverages. The teapot will push more steam into the air.

- Add a tabletop waterfall, fountain, or decorative bubbler to your home.

- Set up an aquarium — not only will the fish entertain and relax you, but the tank will also add continuous humidity to your home.

- Buy a humidifier or vaporizer. A room humidifier is fine for a room that can be completely closed off but will be ineffective in a large, open area. Larger humidifiers can add moisture to an entire floor, and some models connect to a furnace to humidify an entire house.

- Install a router in your clothes dryer chute that can vent the moist laundry air into the house. Note that you must monitor the router for safety and make sure the lint trap is clean and in good condition.

Conversely, if you have too much humidity in your home, your plants become susceptible to root rot, mold, mildew, and disease. If you live in a humid summer climate, keep the windows closed and the air conditioner running, because air conditioners remove moisture from the air. You can also install a dehumidifier or use one as a standalone room dehumidifier to remove humidity. Check to see that a damp basement, leaky plumbing, or other structural issues are not making the problem worse.

What your plant is telling you about water

Your plant will give you signs that it is not being watered appropriately; watch for them. If your plant shows these signs, it is being overwatered and might be suffering from root rot, a soil-borne fungus caused by over watering or poor soil drainage:

- Sudden wilting or droopy leaves and stems
- Yellowing of all leaves and poor growth
- Many leaves dropping from the plant that are not dried out
- A sour, damp smell to the soil
- White or yellow mold on the surface of the soil

If your plant shows the following signs, it might need more watering:

- Wilting, droopy leaves and stems
- Pot is lightweight
- Pale soil

- Brown leaf tips and edges
- Many dried-out leaves dropping from the plant

Plants can also tell you other things about the water. As mentioned before, some plants can be damaged by fluoride or chlorine in tap water. The plant will signal this problem through browning leaf tips and edges, though this can also be a sign that the plant is not receiving enough water. If you have confirmed a good watering schedule for the plant, try using a water filter to remove these chemicals from the city water.

A white or yellow, crusty or crystalline deposit on the soil, stem, and pot indicates an accumulation of salts from the water supply, whether from water softeners or local salts in the water. This crusty surface layer can be removed and swapped with clean soil, and the salty deposits can be scraped off the pot and plant. While the salts should not have a damaging effect on the plant, if you see yellowing leaves or brown leaf tips that you cannot pin to any other problem, you will need to take action. Some of these salts can be filtered out with a water filter — check the filter's information for the types of pollutants it removes.

Water with high iron content can stain your pots — as well as sinks, bathtubs, and other appliances exposed to the water. However, this is usually not a problem for the plants themselves. Again, however, if you see yellowing leaves or brown leaf tips that you cannot attribute to other problems, you will need to change your watering habits. Iron and certain other minerals are not always completely removed by filters, so you may want to purchase distilled water for your plants. Note that some types of distilled water still contain other chemicals like chlorine. Read your labels carefully, and pay attention to your plant's signals.

How Temperature Change Affects Your Plants

Most houseplants come from tropical and subtropical climates, with temperatures similar to those in our homes. These plants thrive with a daytime temperature range of anywhere from 65 to 75 degrees, but they can tolerate occasional summertime highs of up to 90 degrees. They like the same temperature range that average humans find comfortable. At night, houseplants like cooler air, so turn your temperature down by 5 to 10 degrees before bed. This temperature will help your plants produce maximum growth. If you are going to be away on a vacation, make sure that the temperature will remain steady while you are gone.

Windowsill plants cannot tolerate long periods of extreme heat. It is best to increase ventilation through opening a window. Plants actually thrive on fresh air the way humans do. You can also turn on a fan or run the air conditioner to keep the temperature even. Because air conditioning removes humidity from the air, you may want to add humidity to your home as previously discussed, especially in dry climates.

The temperature right next to a window can be quite different from the temperature in the rest of the room. Bright sunlight streaming through a window can increase the temperature by up to 30 degrees 2 inches out from the window. On cold winter nights, the space right next to a window can drop by nearly the same amount. Check your plant's temperature by holding your hand near the window. If the temperature is too extreme, put up a curtain to shield the plant.

Sometimes a change in temperature, along with shorter hours of light, can manipulate the flowering of plants. For example, chrysanthemums produce flowers for longer periods if kept in a cold room — 60 degrees or below — and subjected only to fall or winter daylight. The Christmas cactus begins to flower after a series of short days and low temperatures. Be sure to learn of any such behaviors your plants may exhibit so you can tailor temperatures accordingly.

If you are cooling the air, make sure the air conditioning vent is not adjacent to houseplants so they are not in the path of cold drafts. Plants are also sensitive to hot drafts of air, so make sure your windowsill plants are not directly in the path of a heating vent.

Finally, plants can be sensitive to the heat and oils of our skin. Because our body temperature is around 98 degrees, excessive handling of leaves will damage them and could cause spotting. The stems tend to be less sensitive, so if you must touch a plant frequently, handle it by the stem.

Chapter 7

Plants Cannot Live By Soil Alone

A plant's roots require water, nutrients, and air for optimal growth. Because your windowsill plants will be contained in various sized planters, they will not be able to send roots down through the soil in the ground to get adequate nutrients and water. Ensuring that your plants receive what they need to thrive has now become your responsibility — supply them with the right mix of moisture and nutrients by providing quality potting soil.

Potting Soil: Laying the Foundation

Growing a lush, healthy, and vibrant windowsill garden is like building a house. First, you must lay the foundation, and then you build the house on top of the stable foundation. The "foundation" for household plants is the potting soil. The key to luscious plant growth is a quality soil that is porous and fluffy, providing good drainage but capable of retaining water and nutrients. The soil should be fertile, providing needed nutrients. It also needs to provide coarse particles and aeration for proper root adhesion and growth.

There is a big difference between growing household plants in dirt and growing them in potting soil. Garden soil, or dirt, is a good foundation for plants living outdoors. It remains loose and crumbly thanks to the microorganisms, earthworms, and a variety of insects that constantly move inside it and promote the composting of organic matter. When outdoor soil is used in indoor pots, it hardens like a rock and does not allow roots to establish and grow. It is difficult to maintain an environment conducive to healthy plant growth.

Historically, when this type of soil was all that was available, only hearty and rugged plants could be grown indoors in regular dirt. To remedy this problem, potting soil mixes were developed and marketed to provide a better growing medium. The potting soils available were mostly a garden soil and sand mixture, which was not much better than regular garden soil. To improve on these mixes, pasteurization of the soil was introduced to better control the growing environment and to keep out unwanted microorganisms. Additionally, fertilizer was added to provide better plant nutrition. Most houseplant growers added sand and rocks to the soil for better drainage.

Modern potting soils were developed in the 1970s with the introduction of artificial potting soil mixes. In reality, modern potting "soil" contains little, if any, actual soil. Today, potting soil mixes contain growing media such as peat moss, composted bark, coconut fibers, vermiculite, and/or perlite; please see the "Making your own potting soil mixes" section of this chapter for a detailed breakdown of each material. These organic and inorganic materials act like outdoor soil without the problems associated with it. These mixtures provide nutrients from slow-release fertilizers, moisture, drainage, aeration, and particle matter for root attachment and growth.

Selecting the best potting soil for your windowsill plants

The potting soil or media for indoor plants needs to be of good quality, one that provides nutrient and water retention, root aeration, and drainage.

There are many commercially available mixes that will do a good job for your windowsill plants. The higher-quality mixes contain slow-release fertilizers that provide nutrient availability for a fast start, lasting for the first few months. The mix should include a quality organic base such as peat moss, composted soil, or coconut fiber, as well as soil amendments such as perlite, sand, or vermiculite. If the mix contains peat moss, be certain that the pH level — the measure of acidity or alkalinity — has been adjusted to meet the needs of the plants you want to grow. Peat moss is highly acidic, so alkaline adjustment will be needed. Commercial mixes are somewhat expensive and can contain unnecessary ingredients. It might be better to make your own artificial mix.

There is a potting soil mixture for that?

Today, there are so many different types of potting soil mixes available. There seem to be as many different soil mixes as there are plant varieties. For windowsill plants, any of the commercially made potting soils are adequate. You can also opt for a soilless mix — a medium containing no soil, but rather a combination of organic and inorganic materials. The benefit to using a soilless mixture is that it decreases the chance of harmful fungi and bacteria commonly found in soil. Soilless mixtures are also referred to as "sterile" soil.

Choose mixes that are one part peat moss (or other compost material), one part perlite (or clean sand), and one part vermiculite. Limestone is often added to reduce the acid level if peat moss has been incorporated into the mix. Specialized mixes are recommended for cacti and other succulents, African violets, terrarium varieties, orchids, and bromeliads. A brief description of each specialized mix is listed below:

- **Cactus mix** — Cacti and succulents grow just fine in standard artificial soilless mixes, though many people prefer to use a cactus mix. These blends are made from one part sand — rinsed well with clear water — and two parts soilless mix. The coarse sand provides for quick drainage for those plants that like their moisture in fast gulps followed by dry periods.

- **African violet mix** — African violets prefer a mix high in peat moss. This mix provides a more acidic medium for healthy growth. A basic African violet blend includes equal parts of soilless mix, perlite (or clean sand), vermiculite, and sphagnum peat moss.

- **Terrarium or bottle garden mix** — Terrarium mixes are not as commercially available anymore because terrariums have gone out of fashion in recent years. A good blend would be equal parts of soilless mix, sand (or perlite), vermiculite, sphagnum peat moss, and charcoal chips. The charcoal is added to absorb toxins that can be produced in the soil, especially in the moist, closed environment of terrariums or bottles.

- **Orchid mix** — Orchids are the exception to the rule that a basic soilless mix will work for most plants. Orchids are plants born to live on tree branches and trunks. Their roots are exposed to air to absorb moisture. Orchid mixes should contain higher concentrations of bark compost fragments or coarsely chopped bark and sphagnum moss. Due to the orchid's specialized needs, use a commercially made orchid mix.

- **Bromeliad mix** — Similar to orchids, bromeliads require unique soil for optimal growth and health. Bromeliads grow on trees and absorb their nutrients and water through their leaves and the stiff overlapping leaves called the cup. They do not rely on their roots for feeding. Use a mixture of equal parts of peat moss, perlite (or sand), and chopped tree bark or pine needles. The bark or needles create a more acidic environment well-suited for bromeliads.

Most houseplants grow well in a slightly acidic soil — a pH range between 6.5 and 7.0. The acidity of the soil is determined using the pH scale (0.0 – 14.0), which measures how acidic or basic a substance is. The lower the number in the range is, the more acidic the substance. The higher the number in the range is, the more basic the substance. The most common soil used for your windowsill plants will fall in the range of 6.0 to 6.9 pH, with 6.5 as the average. Some plants grow well in potting mixes with higher acid levels ranging from 5.0 to 6.0. These mixes are either higher in peat moss and bark/pine mulch, or they have been supplemented with acids such as powdered sulfur. Examples of plants that prefer a higher acid level include:

- Azalea (*Rhododendron spp.*)
- Camellia (*Camellia*)
- Calamondin orange (*Citrofortunella mitis*)
- Gardenia (*Gardenia ellis*)
- Hydrangea (*Hydrangea macrophylla*)
- Elkhorn fern (*Platycerium bifurcatum*)
- Zebra plant or saffron spike (*Calathea zebrina*)

There are a handful of plants that need a more neutral pH, or can even grow in potting mixes with higher alkalinity. Alkaline mixes tend to have added limestone, in the form of powdered dolomite limestone. Plants that prefer a neutral pH include:

- Cacti and succulents (*Cacti spp.*)
- Geranium (*Pelargonium spp.*)

- Maidenhair fern (*Adiantum pedatum*)

- Purple passion plant (*Gynura aurantiaca*)

- Spider plant (*Chlorophytum comosum*)

- Swiss cheese plant (*Monstera deliciosa*)

- Wandering Jew (*Tradescantia spp.*)

Commercial potting soil mixes

Huge varieties of commercial potting soils are available on the market today. These products can be found in just about any home and garden section, nursery, hardware store, or grocery/drug store. There are hundreds of brands of commercial and private-label potting soils available. For example, one major national manufacturer markets nine different mixes — potting, moisture control, organic, desert plants, African violets, orchids, high perlite, seed germinating, and sphagnum peat moss for homemade soils. One major advantage to commercial potting soils is that they are properly sterilized and free from pests.

Many gardeners and organic growers will argue that you should make your own potting soil mix. Most university cooperative extension services provide "recipes" for making your own potting soil. Organic gardeners would also recommend making your own mixes using certified organic ingredients. This option is beneficial if you are growing indoor vegetables or herbs. The reality is that for most windowsill plant gardeners, the commercial mixes work just fine.

Here are some tips for buying commercial potting soil mixes:

- Buy only products labeled as potting soil or potting mix, with "houseplants" indicated on the label.

- Do not use mixes labeled as "topsoil" or "garden soil," which are too dense or heavy for windowsill plants.

- Check the label if you need a guide for how much potting soil to purchase. The label will indicate how much of the product is needed to fill containers of various sizes. Always buy a little more than you think you will need.

- If you are growing specialized plants, look for the appropriate mix for plants, such as African violet, orchid, or bromeliad blends.

- Potting soil with insecticides can be helpful for the windowsill gardeners. Do not use on edible plants like chamomile, calamondin orange, rosemary, or other herbs.

It is recommended that you store unused potting soil in airtight containers. The best containers to use are plastic bags with zipper closures. If you do not have these bags, use tape or chip clips to keep the bag airtight. This type of storage keeps the mixture moist and prevents the introduction of microorganisms into the mix. Only buy as much potting soil as you will use within six months to a year.

Making your own potting soil mixes

If you would rather go the organic route, making your own mixtures is fairly easy, and ingredients are readily available at most garden centers. Aside from your mixtures being more organic than commercial blends, making your own potting soil allows you to know exactly what is going into the mixture. Although initially the ingredients may not be very economical, once you learn what goes into your preferred mix, you can begin searching for cheaper sources for ingredients. Over time, as you become accustomed to making your own mixtures, it can prove to be a more economical option.

The basic combinations include a 30-30-30 mixture ($^1/_3$ equal parts) of pasteurized soil or finished compost, sand or perlite, and peat moss.

- **Peat moss**: The basic ingredient in soilless mixes is sphagnum peat moss. Peat moss is partially composted sphagnum moss. The peat moss is harvested from bogs, mainly in Michigan and Canada. Sphagnum peat moss has a highly acidic pH level ranging from 4.0 to 5.0. This organic material tends to have few nutrients and is used to lighten the soil so that roots can spread freely. Peat moss is sterile for houseplants due to the high acid level. The advantage of peat moss is that it provides excellent aeration and holds moisture and nutrients well. The disadvantage is the highly acidic pH level. An alkali such as ground limestone should be added to balance the pH level of the mixture. Sphagnum peat moss should be loosely separated, rather than pulled apart into fine bits; if the peat moss is too loose, it will lose its aeration and moisture retention properties.

- **Vermiculite**: This product is the small flakes of shiny material you often see in flowerpots. It is made from expanded mica that has been sterilized. These are naturally occurring mineral deposits that are heated to expand into a lightweight, plate-like structure. The large amounts of air, water, and nutrients needed for plant growth can be absorbed by mica and released as needed. Its pH is between 6.5 and 7.2. Vermiculite is sold in four particle sizes. The larger-sized particles should be used because they give better soil aeration. Vermiculite can sometimes become compacted over time. Often it is mixed with perlite to prevent packing. Vermiculite is available under many trade names and is sold in most garden centers.

- **Perlite:** This material is created by volcanic rock that has been superheated and sterilized. The resulting product is a lightweight, porous material that looks like small, white polystyrene foam puffs. It is used as an aeration product in potting soil mixtures, just like peat moss; it also does not contain many nutrients, and it does not have the water absorption qualities of vermiculite. Perlite has a pH range between 7.0 and 7.5. Some plants suffer from fluoride burn from perlite, indicated by brown leaf tips and edges that gradually move inward on the leaves. To prevent fluoride burns, add lime to the soil mix; if this does not help, discard the potting soil and use one that does not contain perlite. Some manufacturers add actual foam puffs instead of perlite.

- **Sand:** The larger particle size of sand is useful because it improves drainage and aeration. Water quickly flows through sand, making it ideal for cacti and succulents. Sand can be used in place of vermiculite or perlite, but it will tend to dry out quicker in these mixes. The heavier weight of sand can help to steady a pot, but it cannot store minerals or moisture. You will need to be careful when fertilizing potting mixtures containing high levels of sand. Always thoroughly rinse river sand or play box sand to remove excess salt concentrations and other contaminants.

- **Composted materials:** Bark, pine needles, and other plant materials that are partially decomposed, or composted, are excellent for the organic portion of your mix. Most composted plant materials for use in soil mixtures come from the lumber and food processing industries. These by-product are recycled and used as compost.

Crushed eggshells are a good source of minerals, add coarse material, and can help reduce acid levels. Alfalfa meal is made from alfalfa, a green manure crop containing nitrogen, phosphorous, and potassium.

- **Charcoal**: Charcoal chips or briquettes can be used to absorb toxins that can develop during plant decomposition. It also removes the acidity from the soil.

- **Limestone**: Limestone is a sedimentary rock composed of calcium carbonate. Crushed or powdered limestone can be added to reduce the acidity of the soil mix.

- **Other minerals**: Rock phosphate, a sedimentary rock containing high amounts of phosphate, and gypsum, a soft mineral composed of calcium sulfate dehydrate, can be added to mixes as slow-release fertilizers. Most often, a little limestone is all that is needed if a commercial fertilizer mix is going to be used.

Below are some basic recipes for making your own mix. Modify as you see fit; just ensure that the materials you use are suitable to serve your plant's needs.

All-purpose soilless formula:
A good all-purpose mix will suffice for most common windowsill plants, unless otherwise specified.
   1 part sphagnum peat moss
   1 part medium- to coarse-grade perlite
   1 part medium-grade vermiculite
   ¼ cup per gallon of powdered dolomite limestone mixture

Mixed fertilizer, such as 8-8-8, per manufacturer recommended amounts

Non-peat moss, all-purpose soilless mix:

This is a good all-purpose mix to use when your plant's soil should not contain peat moss.

2 parts compost

2 parts coir (coconut fiber)

1 part vermiculite

1 part blend of washed sand and alfalfa meal

Cactus mix:

Cacti have special needs for optimal growth and health. The following mix will provide the proper drainage and nutrients that cacti love.

1 part sand

2 parts basic soilless mix

African violet mix:

A simple African violet blend includes equal parts of soilless mix, perlite, vermiculite, and sphagnum peat moss.

1 part soilless mix

1 part perlite

1 part vermiculite

1 part sphagnum peat most

Bromeliad mix:

Bromeliads thrive in a humus-rich soil that drains well.

1 part peat moss

1 part perlite

1 part chopped tree bark or pine needles

Orchid mix:

Orchid mixes should contain high concentrations of bark compost fragments, coarsely chopped partially decomposed bark, sphagnum peat moss, or other well-aerated organic materials. No potting soil is used in this mix.

1 part sphagnum peat moss

6 parts fir bark

1 part medium-grade charcoal

Terrarium mix:

A good blend is made by mixing equal parts of all-purpose soilless mix, sand (or perlite), vermiculite, sphagnum peat moss, and charcoal chips.

1 part all-purpose soilless mix

1 part sand or perlite

1 part vermiculite

1 part sphagnum peat moss

1 part charcoal chips

Be aware that buying the separate ingredients for these mixes can cost more than purchasing a commercially produced and blended mix. However, making your own blend allows you to be sure of the ingredients that make up the foundation for your windowsill plants.

Preparing the soil and potting your windowsill plants

Before potting your plants, there are a few more steps you must take. The first is to ensure that your soil has been treated. If you are using a commercially prepared potting soil, this has already been done for you. If you are making your own blend at home, you will want to pasteurize your soil; this is a process of heating a substance at a certain temperature for a certain period of time to kill microorganisms without changing the chemistry of the substance. Heating the soil to a temperature of 180 degrees will kill any diseases, pests, and weeds that may be in the soil. This can be done at home with either a conventional oven or a microwave oven. Be forewarned, however, that the odors emitted during this process may not be pleasant. It is best to do this outside if possible, or in a well-ventilated area.

To pasteurize your soil in an oven, preheat your oven to 180 degrees. Wet the soil and place it in a deep oven-safe pan or roaster — glass or metal will work best. Level out the soil to an even depth of 4 inches. To determine even heat penetration at the end of the processing time, bury a small potato (about 1 or 2 inches in diameter) in the middle of the pan. Put a tight covering of aluminum foil over the pan. In a central area of the soil, but not close to the potato, insert the bulb end of a meat or candy thermometer. Put the pan in the oven and heat the soil for 30 to 45 minutes. Do not overcook the soil. Remove the pan and let the soil cool completely. Check the potato; it should be completely cooked, which indicates the soil has been pasteurized evenly.

If you want to pasteurize your soil in the microwave, wet 2 pounds of moist soil and place it in a plastic bag or container. Leave the bag open, or loosely cover the plastic container, and put the soil in the center of your microwave oven. Set your microwave to about 650 watts. Cook for about two minutes on full power. After pasteurizing the soil, close the bag or container and allow the soil to cool before removal.

If you plan to mix your own soil blends, soil pasteurization should be a routine part of your soil preparation. Pasteurization allows the soil to be heated to an optimal temperature known for killing off harmful organisms while leaving the beneficial ones intact. Using this process will give your plants a healthy foundation to let down their roots.

The mixtures above should let the windowsill plants establish strong root structures. The roots must be strong for the plants to be healthy, and soil that does not compact easily is the best way to ensure the roots can establish themselves.

Place several layers of rock, and sand if you wish, in the bottom of the pot to provide for drainage. The sand can be mixed in with some soil to give an even finer level of drainage control. You can also use some broken charcoal briquettes at the bottom of the pot.

Add the soil to the pot. Fill the pot about halfway before adding the windowsill plants. The soil does not need to have a specific pH balance or exact acidity level unless the plants are tropical or as previously indicated.

Vital Nutrients for Your Plants

Windowsill plants are no different from any indoor or outdoor plants; they need proper nutrition to grow and thrive. There are three primary plant nutrients required: nitrogen; phosphorous, in the form of phosphoric acid; and potassium carbonate, also known as potash. Nitrogen gives plants a healthy green leaf color and good growth. Phosphorous helps build strong root systems, providing for good water and nutrient absorption, especially for flowering plants and for producing seeds. Potash helps plants to better absorb nutrients, resist many plant diseases, and decrease damage from disease and insects.

There are a wide variety of types and combinations of fertilizers available commercially for indoor plants. A myriad of national brand names and private label garden center brands sell many different fertilizer types and nutrient sources on the market today. Names can be misleading, so always check the label for the amounts of actual nitrogen, phosphorous, and potash available as soluble nutrients. There is also a wide range of nutrient balances in the blended fertilizers. Often the blend will be something such as

10-10-10, 5-10-5, or 7-6-19. These numbers refer to the amounts of available elemental nutrients available. In the first example, 10-10-10, there are ten units of nitrogen, ten units of phosphate, and ten units of potassium in the blend. Not only are there a wide variety of types of fertilizers, but fertilizers also come in many different forms. Commercially available products are in the form of crystalline powder, granules, tablets, or even liquid.

It is always important to follow label directions to prevent over-application of the fertilizers. Some products need to be further diluted prior to application. The amount of fertilizer and the frequency of its application depends on the overall health of the plant, rate of growth, age, and vitality. Fertilize only as often as is necessary to attain satisfactory growth and a healthy appearance. It is important not to overuse fertilizers. Each plant's needs vary, whether you should wait every couple of weeks or even months between fertilization. Analyze the condition of each plant prior to applying fertilizer. It is best to fertilize when the plants are healthy and the growing conditions are best for growth and flowering. A good rule of thumb is to apply every two to three weeks in the late spring and summer months when there is more daylight and warmer temperatures. Avoid fertilizing in the winter when there is less light and lower air temperatures. During this time of year, fertilization can harm a plant more than help it. With cooler temperatures, decreased sunlight intensity, and less moisture in the air, plants can go into a dormant state. This dormancy slows their growth and prevents the plant from adequately processing the extra nutrients from the fertilizer. If you must fertilize during the winter, ensure that it is done in very small doses, such as ⅛ to ¼ of the amount recommended on the product label.

Understanding the various types of fertilizer

It is first important to know that plants can grow well without any added fertilizer at all. Plants get many of the minerals they need from water, air, and the nutrients in the potting soil. Plants can actually suffer from over-fertilization. It is possible that more plants suffer from over-fertilization than from under-fertilization. Over-fertilized plants can grow spindly and oversized but are fragile. They can also grow more slowly and fail to flower. Plants weakened by over-fertilization are also more susceptible to insect and microorganism damage. If roots are over-fertilized, they can die off. The plant then shows signs of this damage by the tips of the leaves turning brown, yellow, or even dropping off completely. Over time, an over-fertilized plant can rot at the root's base and die.

Moderate use of fertilizer is the key, especially with smaller windowsill plants. It is recommended that you use about half of the label recommendation of a fertilizer blend. Most manufacturers put the maximum dosage of fertilizer on the label. Windowsill plants do not need anywhere near the amount recommended by most fertilizer manufacturers.

Commercial blends

Most commercial "plant foods" are blends of nitrogen, phosphorous, and potash. These fertilizer combinations are most commonly synthetic fertilizers. Plant fertilizers are packaged as all-purpose plant foods or specialty foods. Specialty blends are for plants such as African violets, orchids, or other blooming plants. These plant foods are equal percentages of nitrogen, phosphorous, and potash, such as 10-10-10. Other specialty blends can be designed for healthy new growth or to relieve nutrient deficiencies. These blends would be higher in nitrogen, such as a 25-10-10. This combination will promote rapid growth, because nitrogen is vital for producing chlorophyll and allows plants to more readily absorb light — the plant's energy source.

Synthetic plant fertilizers come in convenient forms like granules, tablets, liquids, and spikes. They are all dissolved in water. Granules are easy to use because you sprinkle them on the surface.

Tablets are convenient, but the performance is inconsistent. Often, the tablets do not dissolve at a consistent rate, and the fertilizer will not spread well. Liquids are convenient and offer the advantage of watering the plant while you are fertilizing it. Powders used to make liquid fertilizer have the same advantages but can be messier. Spikes are the easiest and most convenient to use. They have some of the same disadvantages as tablets.

Synthetic fertilizers are good for the most exact plant feeding and are convenient to use. They are not as good for the environment, however. They also do not add needed organic matter to the potting soil.

Natural or organic fertilizers

Organic fertilizers are an attractive option, especially for edible windowsill plants such as herbs. Organic plant foods can be excellent sources of nitrogen. They are better for the soil because they add needed organic matter to the potting soil, which assists in composting. The nutrients in these natural fertilizers are slowly released for long-term healthy plant growth. The following are good sources of natural fertilizers: blood meal, cottonseed meal, cow manure (composted and sterile), and fish emulsion. These organic nitrogen sources are available at most garden centers.

There are also other organic fertilizers that provide phosphorous and potassium. For example, bone meal, a mixture of crushed and coarsely ground bones, is an excellent source of phosphorous. Granite meal (finely ground granite rock), greensand, and wood ash are sources of potassium. There are commercially manufactured organic blends that supply all three major nutrients.

One drawback to natural or organic plant foods is that the concentrations of the nutrients can be variable and difficult to determine without testing. They do not smell bad, with the exception of fish emulsion. Organic fertilizers have a slow-release property that provides nutrients to the plant over a longer period of time, reducing nutrient loss due to leaching. However, if the fertilizer is not applied to the soil quickly enough, there will not be enough time for the nutrients to break down and become available to the plant. Be prepared for more long-term care and feeding of your windowsill plants with natural/organic fertilizers.

Micronutrients or trace minerals

Most fertilizer blends contain small quantities of minor nutrients. The three most commonly needed minor nutrients are calcium, sulfur, and magnesium. Even though these are often included in fertilizer blends, these elements are available in sufficient quantities in most potting mixes and from municipal water.

Many plants need trace elements also called micronutrients. A number of the more common trace elements are added to commercial fertilizers. These trace elements include iron, copper, manganese, molybdenum, chlorine, boron, zinc, and nickel. Using a complete fertilizer blend with trace elements — or micronutrients — once or twice a year should be sufficient enough to prevent any signs of deficiencies. Some of the more obvious signs are stunted growth, deformities of the leaves or stems, and leaves with unusual spots that are yellow, red, or even purple.

Some fertilizers use "chelated" trace elements. A chelated mineral is specially treated to allow for better absorption. In this natural process, the treated minerals bind to amino acids; it is this bond that makes the minerals easier for the plant to absorb. Such fertilizers are more expensive but offer more immediate results, which can be beneficial if you have a sick plant.

Recognizing and Treating Salt and Mineral Accumulation

Salt buildup — often called the secret killer — is a common problem for windowsill plants because their growth is limited in a container. The primary culprits are the dissolved minerals naturally occurring in everyday tap water. The buildup of minerals in the form of soluble salts in the soil can damage windowsill plants because as soluble salt levels increase, it becomes more difficult for the plant to extract water from the soil.

When minerals from fertilization or from the water itself dissolve, the soluble salts are formed. After the water is gone, the soluble salts remain in the soil, migrating to the surface and forming a white, crusty layer. This buildup is the result of the minerals and salts remaining after the water in the soil evaporates.

Often, not only will you see the white layer on the soil surface, but there could also be mineral deposits on the surface of the pot — particularly clay pots — at the level of the soil. You will see deposits forming on drain holes as well. In some cases, the entire external surface of a clay pot can form these deposits. As the level of minerals in the form of soluble salts increase in the soil, it becomes more difficult for the plant to take in enough water. Excessive concentrations of salt can become toxic to the plant roots because they will draw water out of the roots. If enough of this water stripping happens, the plant can be severely stunted or even die. Common symptoms include leaf dropping or loss; curled or wilted leaves and foliage; yellow or brown on the edges of the leaves; and slow growth.

You can even see damage to the tips of the roots. It can be difficult to diagnose this condition versus other plant parasites, insects, or diseases with similar symptoms. The visible mineral/salt accumulations on the soil or the pot combined with these symptoms are a good indicator of the problem. The more toxic condition of this soil causes the plant to be weaker, and weaker plants are more susceptible to disease and parasite infestation. Root rot is a common symbiotic disease with these soil conditions.

It is important to water your windowsill plants properly to prevent root rot from occurring. Ideally, when you water there will be enough drainage to fill the drain pan. The excess water in the drain pain indicates that the soil is saturated with a sufficient amount of water. Thoroughly watering your plant in this way will help wash the soluble salts out of the soil. Be sure to empty the drain pan so the pot is not sitting in the drained water. Otherwise, the soil will reabsorb the drain water, which will pull the salts back into the soil. This situation is especially true with clay pots because absorbing the minerals is possible directly through the wall of a clay pot.

A cure for salt and mineral buildup

An effective method of treating mineral and soluble salt buildup in soil is leaching. To leach a plant, pour a large amount of water into the soil and allow the water to drain thoroughly. Leaching will require two to two and a half times the volume of the plant's pot. For example, if a pot will hold a quart of water, then 2 to 2 ½ quarts of water should be used for leaching. When adding the water, do so at a slow rate that will not wash away soil from the top of the pot but is fast enough so that drainage begins in a few minutes. Keep water flowing so the drainage washes away the excessive minerals and soluble salts. If the white, crusty layer has formed, then remove a small amount of the topsoil — up to ¼ inch — to remove the salt layer. Do not add additional soil unless it is necessary.

On the average, plants should be leached every six months. Reduce this process to four-month intervals if the buildup is bad. If you are going to fertilize and it is time for a leaching, you must leach first and fertilize afterward. That way the fertilizer will not be washed out before being utilized by the plant. Good light and drainage allow a plant to tolerate a higher level of salts. If you are not certain if a plant from a nursery or garden center has been leached, it is best to leach it when you bring it home.

If there is an extremely large buildup of minerals and soluble salts due to over-fertilization or improper watering, the best option is to simply repot the plant rather than attempt to correct the soil nutrient balance. The level and speed at which the salt builds up will depend solely on your ability to keep proper drainage in the plant's soil.

Understanding the effects of salt and mineral buildup can help you minimize, prevent, and treat it when it occurs; this same knowledge can help you make better selections of the containers you use for your plants.

Chapter 8

Container Essentials and Garden Designs

One of the most fun parts of creating a windowsill garden is selecting the containers for each plant. The pots allow you to enhance your décor and also provide your plant with a healthy home. Decorating with houseplants is an exciting way to add life and color to your windowsill.

This chapter will show you how to choose the right container for a plant and will also detail the benefits and disadvantages of specific types of pots. You will learn how to group plants for the best effect, arrange foliage types for maximum beauty, and understand how color and texture add excitement to a garden. You will also learn how to set up your windowsill for your new garden home, according to your gardening plan.

Things to Consider When Searching for the Right Container

When choosing the container for each plant, you will need to consider several factors: the size and proportion of the container, the pot material, the ideal pot type for your plant, and the right appearance of the container. Plant containers should be pleasing to you, harmonious with your room, and healthy for your plants.

CASE STUDY: INDOOR SPECIALTY GARDENS

Ellen Covne
Custom Garden Designs, LLC
Wynnewood, PA
www.customgardensllc.com

I got started with windowsill plant gardening through a business network group. The group asked me to prepare an indoor pot as a condolence gift for a member who had suffered a death in his family. From that one event, I went on to offer indoor specialty gardens as part of my landscaping business. Each of my indoor specialty gardens is adapted to the special requests of the person who commissions the garden. Then, I tailor it to the interests — color, fragrance, and textures — of the recipient.

I love to create indoor specialty gardens that have a unified theme. For example:

1. I have used a wooden box with a slate (blackboard) side. These gardens usually go in the kitchen, and the blackboard is a good place to leave messages.

2. I designed a new baby basket in a clear plastic container with

pebbles in the bottom. I put the plant inside a plastic container inside a woven basket that had a pretty liner using baby girl colors. Around the outside of the basket, I wrapped a hypoallergenic throw/blanket/floor mat in a girly pattern for the baby to use. Each

item was designed for reuse later, such as a place to hold stuffed animals, toys, or other items.

3. I also created a kitchen herb garden design using a glass casserole and lid — again, the lid was underneath — and sat it in a black lacy metal type basket. It looked fantastic!

For each indoor specialty garden design, I provide care instructions, identifying the plant and how it likes to be treated. All plants in an indoor specialty garden have compatible needs for soil, water, and light. Because the most common cause of houseplant death is overwatering, I am very specific about how much to water and how often; these instructions also include tips for identifying overwatering and under watering. One client described these instructions as "idiot proof."

Allow for proper drainage

Any plant container should allow proper drainage. Many pots have drainage holes at the bottom to ensure that the soil does not become waterlogged and generate root rot. If your pot does have drainage holes, be sure that you place a saucer or drainage plate under the plant to catch excess water, and dump the collected water after the plant has had an hour or so to absorb what it needs. To protect your windowsill, put a cork liner or protective felt under the saucer. The liner will help prevent water stains or scratches on your sill.

Decorative containers often do not have drainage holes; you have several options to help your plant with proper drainage. Using the decorative container as an outer pot, or "cachepot," and putting the plant in a plain pot with drain holes inside will allow for drainage from one pot to the other. Increase the drainage by setting a layer of small pebbles, gravel, or sand in the bottom of the cachepot. Whenever you use sand, be sure to buy river or lake sand rather than sea sand. The mineral content in sea sand can be toxic to many plants.

Pots without drainage holes can also become drainage-friendly by placing a thick layer of sand, gravel, or crushed clay at the bottom of the pot before filling it with potting soil. When the plant is watered, the excess water will drain down below the roots and into the drainage medium. Plants in this type of container will need much less water because the water that flows to the bottom will take some time to evaporate.

Finally, consider planting foliage with low moisture needs in pots without drainage holes. Because you will water these plants on an infrequent basis and the roots tend to cluster near the top of the soil, the lack of drainage will not be an issue.

Choosing the right container for your plant

When you select a container, you need to consider the right size for the plant you will put in the pot. The container you choose should match the size of your plant; put small plants in small containers, and grow large plants in large containers. Plants too small for their containers will look odd and out of proportion. The soil will remain moist for too long, and the roots can be damaged. If a plant is too large for its container, it will also look out of proportion. The roots of these plants quickly fill the pot, and the pot will dry out quickly. These plants often topple over because their pots do not have enough weight to hold them up. A good guideline is to make sure the plant is more than twice the height of the pot or one and a half times as wide.

The shape of the pot is also an important consideration. For example, tall, narrow containers will need lighter soil that drains easier than short, wide containers that spread moisture more evenly. Larger pots will need less watering than smaller pots. Light pots can simply topple if the foliage is heavier than the pot. Make sure the size and shape of your pot does not interfere with its sunlight requirements by blocking out sun or allowing sunlight to hit too much of the plant. Finally, make sure you match the shape of the root (wide or long) to the shape of the pot.

Common containers

The type of material and shape of the pot can make a big difference to your plant and your décor. Common container materials include clay or terra-cotta, porcelain, ceramic, plastic, and wood. Each type has advantages and disadvantages, and some plants are better suited to one material than another.

The most common indoor plant pot is made from terra-cotta. Terra-cotta pots have an earthy, orange color. The words terra-cotta mean "baked earth" in Italian, derived from the Latin terra cocta. These pots are made from mineral-rich clay. They have one hole in the bottom to allow water to drain out. Because of this, a saucer will be needed under the pot in your home. If you forget the saucer, you will have quite a mess on your floor. Once you have the pot, you can feel free to paint it yourself to match your decorative style. Terra-cotta pots are inexpensive, and their earth tones provide a casual look to your plant. They are available in a number of sizes, from 3 inches to 2 feet in diameter. These types of pots are somewhat porous, so water will evaporate more quickly from these materials. For this reason, these pots make excellent containers for desert plants. If you will be potting non-desert plants, before you use one of these pots, soak it in water overnight so that the clay is suffused with water — otherwise, it will absorb water from the plant's roots.

The advantage of a terra-cotta pot's porosity is that air can reach the roots easily. However, these pots also absorb minerals effortlessly, leaving white stains on the sides of the pot, and mold and mildew can form after prolonged exposure to high humidity. Alternatively, you can buy a clay sealant at craft stores and paint it on the inside and/or outside of the pot. Make sure it is dry, and then wash the pot before use. If you have children, it can be fun to enlist their help in designing pots for the garden by painting them. Buy paints that are safe for clay, and give your children the freedom to decorate the pots for you. They will become more involved in plant care, and you will be encouraging budding green thumbs. Make sure you seal the paint afterward with clay sealant.

Some versions of terra-cotta pots serve a particular purpose. Low, wide pots are used for dish gardens or desertscapes. Strawberry jar planters — a planter designed specifically to grow strawberry plants — have planting pockets on the sides of the jar and a larger opening at top. Some clay pots are shaped like animals or birds, and a rather squat type of pot is used specifically for azaleas. Because these pots absorb water and the edges of the pots are somewhat rough, they are not suited for plants with delicate stems, such as African violets.

A ceramic pot is another more attractive, functional replacement to the generic store-provided pot. These are always glazed because it looks much better and makes the pot stronger. These pots come in a wide variety of sizes. Make sure that you check to see if there is a drainage hole, because this variety of pot does not always have one. If it does not have a hole, it does not mean that you cannot use if for your indoor plants. Just make sure to use it for plants such as citrus trees that do not need drainage holes, or use it as a cachepot.

Glazed ceramic pots tend to be the most expensive type of planting container because they are the most decorative and elegant containers. Ceramic pots can be custom-made to suit your decorating scheme. One disadvantage to using these pots is that they can break easily and do not last long during temperature extremes. For example, pouring cold water into a porcelain pot superheated by the sun on a windowsill can cause it to crack or break.

Aluminum and brass containers are sometimes used for plants, most often as cachepots. These containers hold water well, especially if they are not equipped with drainage holes, and the reflective surface can be pleasing. However, the metal can be discolored by minerals and water, and the bottom of the container can scratch your windowsill.

Baskets can be charming containers for plants. Some baskets are lined with heavy-duty plastic, which does not drain well but does allow you to plant directly into the basket. Unlined baskets can serve as cachepots for plants in other containers, but be sure the inner pot is equipped with a saucer to catch water overflow. One disadvantage of baskets is they are less durable than most other containers, especially after repeated exposure to water; they also absorb mold and disease more readily than other containers.

If you are worried about having your indoor plants in fragile materials such as terra-cotta or ceramics, a pot made out of resin is a good option. Resin is thick and sturdy with a plastic-like feel. It comes in a variety of shapes and sizes to fit almost any need.

Plastic pots are another common container for plants, and they are considered the cheapest type of container. It is likely that your new plants came home in a cheap plastic pot, one not suitable for long-term use. Plastic can come in virtually any color or shape, and these types of containers are versatile. Most plastic pots are equipped with drainage holes and saucers. Plastic is not porous, so you will need to adjust a plant's watering schedule accordingly. An advantage of plastic pots is that they can be more resistant to absorbing mold spores and disease. They are also more durable than many other types of containers.

Glass and terrarium containers can be used to plant small specimens and can include rocks, statuettes, or whimsical scenes. Any kind of glass object with a mouth large enough for inserting plants can be used as a terrarium — old wine jugs, aquariums, vases, or jars, for instance. One advantage of terrariums is that the air remains humid and contains less pollution, and the air temperature remains more stable. However, the greenhouse effect of plants under glass makes them unsuitable for any window with direct sunlight. In addition, plants that suffer under high humidity, such as cacti, or need good air circulation, such as bromeliads, will not grow well in a terrarium.

While the above containers are the most common types of pots, any object that can hold soil is a possible houseplant vessel. Use your imagination as you plan your windowsill garden. To give you some ideas, consider using large seashells, baskets, tabletop water fountains, teacups, vases, hurricane jars, votive candle cups, sealed wooden bowls or boxes, kitchen pans, or hollowed-out rocks. Evaluate the porosity and durability of the container, and make adjustments as previously described to ensure optimum performance. As long as you provide the right care and prepare the container properly, your houseplant will thrive.

Crafting the Ideal Windowsill Location

You might already have a windowsill in mind — or you might dream of a windowsill garden but do not have the ideal shape for a garden. In the past, houses were built with deeper sills, as much as 6 inches deep, to accommodate thicker walls, extra room for storm windows or shutters, and additional storage space.

Newer houses often have small sills or just a thin space between the window trim and the window frame. You might have to make a few modifications before putting up your garden. If there is a narrow sill, you can build out the sill by attaching a board to the protruding sill and using brackets underneath the board to anchor the board to the wall and offer support to the plants. Be sure your hardware is strong enough to hold the weight of your plants. It is wise to paint this shelf with glossy paint to resist water damage and staining. You can also line the shelf with plastic-coated wallpaper, drawer liners, or plastic for protection.

You can also attach shelves directly to the molding around the windows. The same sort of shelf/bracket system described above will also work well for attaching the shelf to molding or even the adjacent wall. If you do not like the look of a wooden shelf or feel it blocks too much light from the room, try wire utility shelves or glass shelves, or search online for clear plastic plant shelves.

If you are lucky enough to have wide sills, your pots can grow directly on the sill. Take the precaution of applying a layer of water-resistant paint to the windowsill to protect it from potential watering spills. You can also protect the shelf by lining it with plastic-coated wallpaper, drawer liners, or plastic.

Some homeowners install a bay window, which is a pre-made extension of the window that extends out from the house. Some of these windows come equipped with shelves, or you can install them yourself. Depending on the construction of the plant window, you will need to put a layer of insulation at the bottom of the window to protect plants from cold. Foam, commercial insulation, or an old towel will work for insulation. You will also need to make sure that the temperature does not become too high or too low for the plants you will keep there. Closed plant windows are most like a small greenhouse; they are a self-contained environment in which light, heat, and moisture is controlled. While this type of plant window can be expensive to set up and takes time to maintain, the effort can be worth it to enjoy rare specimens that require a controlled environment.

If none of these options is possible for your plants, do not give up the window garden idea. Some plant centers stock specially designed windowsill planters. You can also plant several varieties of houseplants in a basket or hanging planter, and suspend it from a hook in the ceiling or a bracket on the wall, or place a vining plant at the space on top of your cupboards and allow it to dangle down the sides of your window.

An Introduction to Windowsill Garden Design

Some grow windowsill gardens for utility purposes — for example, the widely popular herb garden, or a windowsill garden for germinating new seeds. While you should consider design and beauty for all types of gardens, some types of gardens require more effort than others.

Create a work of art with simple design principles

Your windowsill garden can become a work of art through simple design principles and attention to plant arrangement. You should design each arrangement in the context of its planned home; do not just take into account the appearance of the plant itself, but also consider your selected container, the background of the window and the view beyond it, and any of the room's features and furniture around the plant.

Here are a few basic principles along with more advanced ideas to perfect your garden:

- Simple plants will show off ornate pots, while plain pots will better showcase more flamboyant plants.

- If you want a harmonized garden, match the shape of the pot to the shape of the plant. For example, a tall pot will complement a tall, narrow plant.

- If you want to emphasize contrast in shapes, plant a round, thick plant such as a hydrangea in a narrow container.

- The pot should not be taller than the plant.

- To harmonize plant leaf and foliage colors with the pot, choose the same color in different shades, or colors that are near each other on the color wheel — for example, blue, turquoise, and green.

- For drama and impact with the plant and the room, choose contrasting colors — ones that are opposite each other on the color wheel, like purple and yellow.

- If you want to show off a pot, do not plant trailing or weeping plants.

- A grouping of plants with different textures, growing habits, and foliage will stand out in identical pots.

- A grouping of eclectic pots can highlight a set of identical plants.

- Plants provide the most striking visual impact if they are grouped in uneven numbers of, for example, three to five pots.

- Pots can either harmonize with the plant and room — for example, a cactus in a rough clay pot for a casual earth-toned room — or provide focal interest through contrast, such as a wispy trailing plant potted in a painted container of a room with lots of right angles and solid colors.

- Flowering plants in highly patterned containers will compete and look too busy.

- Baskets, wooden cachepots, and terra-cotta pots lend a casual feel to the windowsill.

- Plain white or undecorated clay pots are versatile and give a clean, simple look to your plant grouping.

An arrangement can be as simple as a single plant in a plain container or a more complex, detailed grouping of several plants. When you select plants for display, consider the plant's form — its current shape and how it will look as it grows — as well as the size, shape, color, and texture of its leaves and flowers.

Coordinate your garden with the room theme

Like any interior design project, your windowsill garden or container grouping will have two basic design elements: the bones of the design and the focal points. Sometimes the bones or focal points are dictated by the design in the rest of the room; use a round arrangement as an accent in a sharp-lined room, or a plant with small, frilly flowers on long, airy stems to balance a room with heavy furniture and accessories. Here are some other ideas to create harmony between your room's decorating style and your windowsill arrangement:

Country style — The country look incorporates wicker or overstuffed furniture, floral material, nature-themed accessories, and a casual atmosphere. Try a variety of decorative, slightly rustic pots to complement the room.

Modern — The modern style incorporates clean lines, minimalist furniture and accessories, and the use of marble, steel, and glass. Plants with strong, simple lines work best, such as mother-in-law's tongue, dracaena, or tall cacti. Use minimalist containers, and experiment with brightly colored pots to add a focal point to your plants.

Oriental — This style implements ornate, painted furniture; uses wicker, bamboo, or carved woods; and has many decorative accessories. Exotic plants, such as orchids or bromeliads, string of pearls, or jasmine will enhance the décor. By contrast, a Japanese-themed room might have simple, modern décor with natural fabrics and woods; try adding bamboo, bonsai, or grasses to your windowsill.

Traditional — Ornate English, French, or German classic furniture dominates this style, with equally decorative and upscale accessories such as candle sconces, tapestry rugs, and formal wall coverings. This style is accentuated with soft-contoured, bushy plants like ferns, cyclamen, miniature palms, and gloxinias. Porcelain or ceramic pots in an old-fashioned design will accentuate the plants and décor.

Adding another level of interest to your arrangement

If you are planning to place a number of plants in one container or group several potted plants in an interesting placement, you will have to give further consideration to the design. Think of your foliage as the bones of your container design. Consider the color, texture, and size of the leaves — for example, a frilly-leaved angel-wing begonia for color and texture, grasses for spiky airiness, and a pothos for wide foliage contrast. Have at least one tall/thin plant, one filler, and one trailing plant or tiny-leaved plant. Here are a few other mixed-container ideas:

- Create a focal point within a mixed arrangement by adding special plants with height, bold leaves, or dazzling color.

- Create color harmony and foliage interest by planting several species with the same color foliage but different leaf shapes. If the color is a contrast to the rest of the room, the garden quickly becomes a focal point.

- Create foliage interest by planting several specimens with the same leaf shape but different colors.

If you include garden art, such as a small statue, wire sculpture, whimsical signs, or an interestingly shaped accent rock, your plants will have an extra design element that will catch attention. You can also hang tiny bells or little Christmas ornaments to the stems of plants.

Get creative with your mulch. A tall, spiky plant might be enhanced with a layer of green peat moss over the surface of the soil. Enhance a small, Japanese container with a layer of soft, smooth sand. Try putting a layer of wine corks on top of the soil of a larger plant, or use colored marbles as mulch. Here are a few other creative ideas:

- Rough-textured sand
- Pieces of broken clay
- White quartz gravel
- Colored glass shards
- Coffee beans
- Smooth river stones
- Beach glass (wash well before using)
- Tiny pine cones

- Miniature ground cover plants, like creeping Jenny or Scotch moss

- Colorful twigs

- Small glass Christmas ornaments

Though the primary purpose of mulch is to cover the top layer of soil so less moisture is lost, decorative mulches can add interest and drama to your pots and cover boring soil if your plants are low enough to view it.

Garden Plans

What a joy it can be when you are able to create a smaller indoor replica of your outdoor garden. All of the elements discussed so far — light, water, temperatures, humidity, and soil condition —are critical to the success of your indoor garden. It is equally important, however, to plan your gardens before you pick the proper plants and materials.

Bonsai gardens 101

A bonsai garden is not a garden that you can plant and then merely water and tend — it is an ongoing relationship between you and a long-lived plant or tree. The purpose of raising a bonsai plant is to grow a miniature tree in a specific shape by selective pruning and training branches in a pleasing design. This practice takes years, but the act of carefully managing these plants can be a contemplative, peaceful activity.

Originally, the Japanese grew bonsai in an outdoor garden, but indoor bonsai plants have become enormously popular. The appearance of the foliage and branches are the bulk of the appeal. The Japanese have several traditional shapes for bonsai. One design creates a gnarled miniature tree with an interesting shape that suggests a rugged, windswept climate. Another design accents sculptural branches and trunk with a topknot of foliage. Bonsai plants are often meant to be contemplated from a single direction, so the trimming will accent that particular view.

Bonsai plants can be grouped in one of three categories: evergreens, deciduous trees, or other types of plants, some with flowers. Some types are dwarf varieties of full-sized trees or bushes, while other bonsai are kept in miniature form through pruning and a minimum amount of soil and nutrients that slow the plant's growth. Many specimens can be found in garden stores or greenhouses, but the Internet is also an excellent place to find starter plants. Make sure you understand the plant's requirements before selecting one to train. Here are a few varieties often cultivated as bonsai:

- **Boxwood** — This evergreen bush is an excellent choice for a bonsai, because it easily conforms to any shape. Boxwoods have small, soft, oval-shaped leaves that are a glossy dark green color, though many cultivars are recommended for bonsai specimens. Outdoors, gardeners commonly use full-size versions as accent bushes or hedges.

- **Ficus** — This deciduous plant is grown indoors in a large variety.

  The many cultivars are popular as bonsai because the ficus plant will develop a smooth trunk and mid-sized, almond-shaped leaves. One benefit to this plant is the pliable branches that can be braided, twisted, or easily trained into interesting designs. Ficus plants can grow more quickly than some other bonsai plants. The ficus is also an easy-to-grow specimen.

- **Jade plant** — A common succulent houseplant, this plant makes an interesting bonsai specimen due to its heavy trunk and thick, dark green leaves. It is also hardy and easy for beginners to grow.

- **Juniper** — This evergreen with prickly star-shaped needles is the plant most associated with bonsai. Juniper is a common landscaping plant, but dwarf versions make excellent bonsai. The plant will grow a gnarled, twisted trunk with the branches trained to an interesting design, suggestive of an ancient tree.

- **Maple** — There are several types of this deciduous tree that make

excellent bonsai specimens. A Japanese maple has deeply lobed or feathery, reddish-purple leaves; the trunk and branches naturally grow in interesting shapes. Common maples have the familiar five-lobed leaves. These plants will grow quickly but require partial sun conditions and must be kept evenly moist so that the leaves do not burn or drop.

- **Umbrella plant** — This common houseplant is beautiful as a bonsai because it has many gray branches that can be braided or twisted while young and tender. Each branch ends in a rosette of pointed oval leaves that are dark green and shiny.

Once you have chosen your plant, you will need to keep your bonsai garden in a window with the optimal light conditions for that species. You will also need to water and fertilize it according to its specific needs. In addition, bonsai plants need special care and training; many books have been written on the specific care for bonsai plants. Here are some basic instructions:

- **Pruning** — Using sharp clippers, clip deciduous stems just above the bud in the direction the bud was growing.

- **Root trimming** — At least once during the resting season, the roots should be trimmed back by a third. The best time to trim or "prune" roots is when you are planning to transplant your plant. Trimming the roots reduces the root system so you can repot it into a smaller or same-sized container.

- **Training branches** — Slowly bend branches and trunks into the desired direction. Move the branch a little at a time, and secure the branch in that direction with copper or aluminum wire until it naturally grows in that direction. Do not try to bend the foliage too far at once because you can damage or snap the branches.

- **Watering and feeding** — Bonsai plants need only small amounts of water and fertilizer at a time because their pots have little soil. Plants should be fertilized only in the growing season.

Designing a bonsai garden

You Will Need:

- One 6- to 8-inch ficus plant
- One tray-type container or bonsai pot
- Bonsai wire (5 mm to 6 mm)
- String or twine
- Soil mixture of one part sand to two parts humus
- Sharp miniature clippers
- Bonsai weights (optional)
- Decorative mulch or moss

Fill a bowl with lukewarm water and immerse the plant's root ball for at least five minutes. Allow it to drain. Trim the plant's roots so that it will fit within the tray container with the crown of the root ball under soil. Set the plant in the pot and fill with soil, packing the soil down so that it holds the plant in place. Place mulch over the soil.

Examine the plant for a pleasing shape that naturally emerges from the branches and trunk. You might choose a cascading, upright, angled, or weeping shape for the tree; you can find ideas online at sites such as **www. bonsai-garden.com** or **www.bonsaisite.com**. Once you have an idea for a design, carefully begin pruning off branches that do not conform to the shape. Take a length of bonsai wire and wrap it around a branch, carefully bending it into its desired position. Attach the wire to the trunk for support and then loosely twist it around the branch so that the tree still has some room to grow. To keep the wire and branch in place, tie a piece of twine to the branch and tie the other end to a small stake in the soil.

Alternatively, you can bend a branch by tying a small bonsai weight to the branch with string or twine. When the branch has been fully trained in the direction you want it to move, the weight or wire can be removed.

A bonsai tree is an ongoing project; unless you tire of the project, the tree is never "done." You can continue to shape and prune a bonsai throughout its lifetime.

Desertscape garden

You Will Need:

- One aloe vera plant
- One 2-inch echeveria or jade plant
- One 6x6x3-inch square black pot
- 2 to 3 cups soil mixture of 1 part sand to 2 parts artificial or beneficial soil
- 1 to 2 cups of fine white sand

One of the best reasons to grow a desertscape garden is because of the low-maintenance nature of cacti and succulents. A desert garden can be placed in a sunny window and watered about once a month, or even less, depending on the species. They are designed to look like a natural desert environment using sand, gravel, or other natural mulches as well as rustic pots and accessories. There are thousands of cacti and succulents to choose from, and a gardener can find many small or slow-growing specimens perfect for the tight space of a windowsill.

Because these desert plants have such a variety of shapes and forms, it is fun to group plants with different shapes — such as spikes, rosettes, barrels, and globes — in identical pots, or form a collection of identical plants in pots of varying sizes, colors, and textures. This particular desert garden design incorporates a minimalist Asian design with two small succulents; the result is a Japanese-like sand garden with two slow-growing plants.

Fill the pot with the soil blend and set the plants in the soil so that each root ball is just covered. The plants might look best in a random design; set them far enough apart that they will have a little room to grow. Water the soil sparingly.

Holding the plants steady, pour in the sand to a depth of about ½ inch to ⅔ inch around the plants. Make sure the entire surface of the pot is covered with sand. Using your fingers or a plastic fork, rake the sand smooth. Mist the surface with water using a spray bottle. Add any decorative objects to the pot. This pot can be set in any type of light; the less light it receives, the slower the plants will grow and the paler the color of the plants.

Water sparingly about once a month, or more often if the container has drainage holes. You can check for dryness by inserting a toothpick into the container down to the level of the soil. If soil and sand clings to the toothpick, the pot has sufficient water. Note that the sand will be easily disturbed by watering, so pour the water slowly and do not water in just one place.

Italian herb garden

You Will Need:

- One basil plant, 5 to 6 inches tall
- One oregano plant, 2 to 3 inches in diameter
- One marjoram plant, 2 to 3 inches in diameter
- One creeping thyme plant, 2 to 3 inches in diameter
- One clay pot, or a ceramic pot painted in an Italian design
- Soil of 1 part sand to 2 parts commercial potting soil

When you grow an Italian herb garden on your windowsill, you will never run out of fresh herbs for making spaghetti sauce, pesto, or sauce for a pizza. This design has a rustic feel to it, emphasizing the casual nature of a slow dinner in a Tuscan *trattoria*.

When setting up an Italian herb garden, pair herbs that have similar growing requirements. Basil serves as an upright accent with large leaves, while the marjoram and oregano provide soft, cascading accents with tiny oval leaves. Adding thyme provides the final accent with thin needle-like leaves; thyme and basil can be found in many colors, including variegated and purple-leafed types.

The plants in this garden are sun-lovers. Make sure this garden receives plenty of direct sunlight and a warm temperature. Water when the first inch of topsoil is dry. Oregano, marjoram, and basil will suffer if the soil is allowed to dry out completely, although thyme is a little hardier. To keep your Italian herb garden producing abundantly, continue to harvest from the ends of the plant. Always clip basil from the top to encourage bushiness, and from the upward-protruding stems of other plants to emphasize the cascade over the sides of the pot.

Herbs thrive in a soil that is more acidic, so a pH below 7.0 would be ideal. To give your Italian herb garden a good foundation, prepare an all-purpose soilless formula as described in Chapter 7, or use a ready-made potting soil available at a local nursery or garden center. Fill the container with potting mixture to the neck, at least 3 inches below the rim. Water lightly whenever the topsoil layer is dry.

Water garden

A water garden can bring a peaceful, contemplative touch to a room. The minimalist combination of water and a few floating plants are more beautiful when viewed through an interesting glass container, and this type of garden is the easiest to set up and care for. Choose an interesting container, like a decorative vase, an apothecary jar, a fishbowl, or antique glassware, for a pretty composition. A variety of plant textures and sizes will make the garden even more interesting. But you do not need to stop there. By adding colored glass or marbles, decorative rocks, a water fountain, underwater plants, fish, or sculptural accents, you can turn your water garden into a spectacular focal point for an entire room.

There are many types of water gardens. Depending on the type you design, you might have to add fertilizer to the water, although the right mix of plants and algae might be sufficient. Ask an aquarium or plant expert for the best way to care for the plants. Make sure you understand the sunlight requirements as well. Some plants cannot stand direct sun, and most water garden plants will not tolerate a cold environment.

A garden entirely underwater contains plants like hornwort, eelgrass, or anubias — any type of plant found in stores that sell aquarium supplies. These plants can either drift in the water or root in a layer of aquarium gravel, sand, or decorative rocks. Some plants — such as water hyacinth, marsh marigold, or water lettuce — will float on the surface of the water. Semi-aquatic plants grow best with their roots underwater, but the crown and foliage completely above the surface. Root these plants in sand or gravel. A tropical water garden with bamboo shoots or an umbrella plant in water is an easy-care option for a sunny windowsill. Finally, a bog garden can be an unusual conversation piece. There are many variations in construction and design, but the main characteristic is that they are built in soggy, consistently wet areas. In a natural habitat, bog plants grow in soil with poor drainage, almost an even mixture of water and peaty dirt. Many beautiful plants can grow in this environment — try cape rush, drosera, or mare's tail in a waterproof container of sand, peat moss, and distilled water.

Tray or dish garden

Designing a garden in a shallow, decorative tray or dish — such as a clay pot saucer or a wicker basket — allows you to make the most of an unusual container, which is often the focus of the garden. The container can be any object that fits on your windowsill, from an old serving tray to an ornate antique bowl. A thrift store or garage sale is the perfect place to find a good container with lots of character. These containers do not have any drainage, so selecting the proper soil mix and paying careful attention to watering are key to a successful garden. In addition, the tray or dish must be waterproof and should not be in danger of being damaged by water.

To create the harmonious effect of ornate design, choose a highly decorative container and use plants with flashy colors and small, frilly foliage. If the focus should be on the container, plant a few simple pieces in it; if the focus should be on the plants, choose a modest container for decorative specimens. Conversely, if you have a simple, spare design within your room, your dish garden should incorporate a plain tray with a few understated foliage plants, perhaps ones with simple sculptural interest.

Note that the plants you choose should be ones that can live well together and have similar lighting and watering needs. Because a tray garden is wide but not deep, the plants should not require excessive amounts of room for root development. Before planting, consider the angle at which the garden will be viewed, and arrange the plants to show their most pleasing side in that direction. Try several arrangements until you find the one that suits your garden the best.

Terrarium or glassed-in garden

Terrariums are special gardens consisting of miniature plants and decorative objects within a glass jar, large vase, glass box, lantern, or other glass container. Gardeners design the plants to be viewed from all sides. Plants are chosen for their small, slow-growing natures, which gives the garden the look of a real outdoor garden in miniature form. The containers tend to hold in moisture, so the plants in the garden must be sub-tropical ones that appreciate a warm, humid environment.

Glassed-in gardens often contain fragile or special specimens, such as a tender orchid or fragile ferns, covered with an upside-down glass vase, bell jar, or apothecary jar. This arrangement calls attention to the plant while providing a stable environment and protection. If the air inside the glass becomes too humid or stale, gardeners often use props to lift the bottom of the glass high enough to allow some circulation.

Select plants that have similar environmental needs and match the soil to the needs of the plants. Plants that will remain small, such as button fern, Irish moss, miniature holly, strawberry begonia, or polka-dot plants, are perfect for small terrariums. In a larger container, you might try asparagus fern, English ivy, miniature African violet, or prayer plants.

If you use an aquarium or a large-mouthed container, you will not need any special tools to plant the garden. If you have a small-mouthed jar, try taping a plastic spoon, fork, and cloth to dowel rods and use those as your miniature gardening tools. Then follow these steps to plant your garden:

1. Moisten enough soil to fill the bottom 2 inches of the terrarium. If the container is large, insert a moistened layer of sand or pea gravel before adding the soil.

2. Remove the plants from their pots and plant them according to your planned arrangement. Make sure the entire root ball is covered.

3. Cover up the soil with mulch, such as sphagnum moss, peat, or decorative stones or gravel.

4. Watch the container for fogging in the few days after planting. Fogging or condensation means that there is too much moisture in

the soil. If there is, try to increase circulation around the container. When it only fogs up at night, the soil is properly moist.

The "greenhouse effect" of the glass jar will make the air fairly warm, so be sure not to place the garden in direct sun, and check the temperature from time to time.

Chapter 9

Increasing Your Plant Collection With Propagation

When indoor gardeners become comfortable with caring for their houseplants, it is a natural progression to begin thinking about how to increase their collections. Plants have a tendency to overgrow their own containers, produce "baby" plants, or grow so woody that it easiest just to start over with a new plant. This overgrowing behavior is why it is important to know how to produce new plants from the houseplants on your windowsills.

Propagation, the process of creating more plants from the primary plant, can be fun and rewarding. When you see new shoots springing from seeds you have planted or watch plantlets or roots develop from a parent plant, you cannot help but feel a sense of accomplishment and excitement. *Each plant has its own reproduction method; chapters 2 through 5 described how to propagate each species.* This chapter will discuss the most common propagation methods.

Rooting

Increasing plants through rooting is one of the easiest and most familiar ways to create new plants. Many cuttings of plant parts will develop new roots if set in water, dampened soil, vermiculite, peat moss, sand, or sphagnum. Some plants will live indefinitely in a container of water after roots have developed. They will root even more quickly if you add a few drops of diluted fertilizer to the rooting medium. If you choose not to root in water, make sure the rooting medium is kept moist by watering or misting the topsoil.

Plants grow roots at different rates. English ivy and pothos are two plants that develop roots quickly. Other plants, especially ones with woody stems, can take weeks before the first feathery roots begin to show. One advantage to rooting cuttings in water is that you can easily see the roots' length. If planted in soil, check the roots in several weeks by gently pulling on the plant. If it does not rise from the soil, the roots are sufficiently developed.

Steps for propagating by rooting

1. Begin by using a sharp, clean razor or knife to cut a section of the plant that has a healthy stem and leaves. Make sure the cutting contains at least four to six leaves so that photosynthesis can continue to nourish the plant.

2. Set the plant in the rooting medium; if rooting plants that are susceptible to powdery milder or fungal problems, such as tuberous plants, dust the cut ends with sulfur powder before inserting in the soil or water. Rooting hormone powder applied to the cut stem can also encourage roots to grow in soil, vermiculite, or moss. Sulfur powder and rooting hormone can be found in a garden store or online.

3. Set the cutting in indirect light for a few days before moving it to the plant's usual light location.

4. Allow the roots to grow at least one-third to one-half of the total plant size before setting the plant in a pot with the recommended

potting soil. If the plant has been rooting in a solid medium, make sure some of that material remains on the stem and is mixed with the potting soil. If the plant was rooted in water, pour some of the water into the pot to moisten the soil.

5.   Keep the plant evenly moist and away from bright, direct sunlight until the roots take hold and the plant produces new growth.

Tip Cutting

One major benefit of propagating through tip cuttings is the ability to begin new, healthy plants from old, woody, or poorly performing plants. This method is especially useful for upright or training plants, especially as the plants lose lower leaves and begin to look leggy.

Steps for propagating by tip cutting

1.   Select firm, ripe stems — not too old and woody, nor too young and fragile.

2.   Using a sharp, clean knife or razor, cut a section of stem that is at least 2 inches long and contains four to six healthy leaves. Just as the rooting method described above, these cuttings can be placed in water, dampened soil, vermiculite, peat moss, sand, or sphagnum.

3.   Dust the cut ends of mildew-prone plants with sulfur powder before inserting in the soil or water. Rooting hormone powder applied to the cut stem can also encourage roots to grow in soil, vermiculite, or moss. The plant should be set in the planting medium just deep enough that the bottom set of leaves do not come in contact with the soil.

4. If the cutting is not set in water, mist the plant well and cover it with a clear plastic back to hold in moisture.

5. Set the cutting in indirect light for a few days before moving it to the plant's usual light location.

6. After a few weeks, gently pull on the plant. If it does not rise from the soil, the roots are sufficiently developed.

7. When the roots are sufficiently developed, remove the plastic covering and set the plant in a pot with the recommended potting soil as described above.

8. If the plant has been rooting in a solid medium, make sure some of that material remains on the stem and is mixed with the potting soil.

9. If the plant was rooted in water, pour some of the water into the pot to moisten the soil.

10. Keep the plant evenly moist and away from bright, direct sunlight until the roots take hold and the plant produces new growth.

Leaf Cutting

Leaf cutting can be a fascinating propagation method; some plants have the ability to reproduce by growing new plants along the edges of a leaf in contact with soil. Begonias, African violets, echeveria, jade plants, and Christmas cacti are all examples of plants that can reproduce this way; you can view a more extensive list of such plants at Texas A&M University's Agricultural Extension website (**http://aggie-horticulture.tamu.edu/greenhouse/nursery/guides/ornamentals/prop.html**). Many will produce roots directly through the cut leaf, while others will produce a number of new little plants along the edges of the leaf "parent."

Steps for propagating by leaf cutting

1. Use a clean, sharp knife or razor to cut a healthy, fully formed leaf from the parent plant.

2. Fill a small pot with a rooting material such as vermiculite or commercial rooting soil.

3. Gently press the stem end into the material, and anchor it with a small piece of gravel or bark. Alternatively, mist the leaf with room-temperature water, and then lay the leaf faceup on the surface of the soil.

4. Place a pebble or small piece of gravel on the leaf so the edges and the underside of the leaf stay in contact with the rooting medium.

5. Water the pot, and then cover it with a clear plastic bag, clear drinking cup or bottle, or plastic greenhouse lid. This creates the optimal humidity level and temperature for new plantlets to grow.

6. Mist the surface of the plant if it appears dry. Watch out for any signs of mildew; the cutting will rarely survive if mildew develops. If it does, discard the leaf and rooting material and start over.

7. After new plantlets have developed within several weeks to several months, depending on the species, and each new plantlet has several leaves, cut them from the parent leaf and re-plant each one in its own pot of soil.

8. Water the plants well and gradually introduce them to their windowsill location.

Leaf cutting for begonias

A leaf cutting method that works well for begonias is to:

1. Clip a healthy leaf and lay it faceup in rooting material.

2. With a sharp, clean knife, make a slash along each of the main veins. The new plants will develop along each slash, and after those plants mature, the original leaf can be cut into plant sections.

Rooting Offsets

Offsets are often runners, or long thin stems that grow from parent plants and produce small plantlets; other offsets are small plants that develop on the sides of a mature plant. Examples of such plants are spider plants, African violets, and many types of cacti. Often, these plantlets will form their own root systems while still attached to the mother plant.

Steps for propagating by rooting offsets

1. Many of these plantlets can be snipped directly from the main plant and potted, but if the plantlet is firmly connected to the parent plant, use a sharp, clean razor to divide the plantlet from the parent, keeping as much of the new plant intact as possible.

2. If the cut is a large one, dust it with sulfur powder before planting it in rich potting soil. The sulfur powder encourages more vigorous plant growth.

3. Place the rooting end about ½ inch deep into the soil and water it well.

4. If the plantlet tends to tip over, prop it up with toothpicks or gravel until the roots appear, which should be within several weeks.

5. Keep the soil moist during the rooting period. The rooted plant can remain in the same pot until it outgrows it.

Dividing Roots, Stems, or Tubers

Plants that produce multiple stems, roots, or tubers can be the easiest plants to propagate. Some plants, like spider plants, can be removed from the pot and pulled into separate plants by the root. Make sure each plant has a good percentage of the whole root ball, for example, no less than a third of the whole. Each root division can then be planted in its own pot and watered thoroughly.

Some plants without long stems grow whorls or plant offsets that can be separated from the main plant, similar to rooting offsets. Bromeliads are a good example of this type of plant.

Steps for propagating by dividing roots, stems, or tubers

1. Use a sharp, clean razor to cut off the whorl or new plant stem, keeping as much of the new plant intact as possible without damaging the parent plant.

2. Dust the cut with sulfur powder before planting it in rich potting soil with the roots or cut stem completely covered.

3. Keep the soil moist during the rooting period. The rooted plant can remain in the same pot until it outgrows it.

Some plants that grow from a central tuber produce plantlets from the tuber alongside the main plant. Oxalis and amaryllis are two good examples. To divide these plants, take the plant from the pot and shake the soil from the tuber. Cut the tuber into sections, leaving each plant a good section of the main tuber. Repot each plant and water it well.

If your tuberous plant does not develop additional plantlets, you can divide the tuber itself. A mature tuber will grow eyes, just like a potato. Remove the tuber from the pot and shake the soil away. Cut the tuber into sections with at least one eye per segment. Dust each cut surface with fungicide before repotting.

Planting Seeds

Most flowering plants produce seeds, and a vigilant indoor gardener can collect these as the plant completes a flowering cycle. Alternatively, you can buy seeds from a store or online merchant. Seeds will germinate best in pots or flats filled with peat, sphagnum moss, or special soil for germination.

Steps for propagating by planting seeds

1. Begin by wetting the planting material.

2. Press small seeds onto the soil; larger seeds should be planted at a depth of ¼ to ½ inch. A plastic sheet, glass jar or cup, or greenhouse lid will hold in moisture during the germination period.

3. Place the pots or trays in a warm, low-light area until you see the first sprouts, and then place the pots in a sunny location.

4. Keep the soil evenly moist.

5. When the plants have developed two or three sets of leaves each, remove the lid or plastic, and turn the pots occasionally so the plants will not grow in just one direction.

6. Repot the plants as they begin to mature and crowd each other in the pots.

Planting Bulbs

Bulbs are a catchall name for various bulbous plant parts like corms, rhizomes, or tubers; these come in various sizes, shapes, and growth habits. Each type will develop smaller bulbs as the plants mature, and these can be separated and repotted. Bulbs are sold commercially in a dormant state in packages that allow ventilation so the bulbs do not sprout or become mildewed. Check these bulbs carefully, as some may consist of one large bulb with several smaller bulbs that have started to develop. These can be pulled apart and planted separately.

All bulbs have a root end and a plant end; it is often easier to identify the root end by small roots clinging to that side of the bulb. Obviously, it is important to plant the bulbs right-side up, but many plants can reverse their sprouting direction if planted upside down. Grown from bulbs, plants will develop in six to eight weeks after planting, given the proper conditions.

Steps for propagating by planting bulbs

1. To maintain a healthy, flowering plant, division may be necessary after the first few growing seasons. When the number of flowers and the size of the plant start to decrease, consider separating the bulbs and replanting. Dig up the plant, brush away the dirt from the bulbs, and look for bulblets sprouting off the main bulbs.

2. Gently pull these little ones away from the main bulb, but do not forcefully remove bulbs that are not ready to be separated.

3. Put the bulbs in a container of soil mixed as one part potting soil, one part sand, and one part perlite or peat moss. Several bulbs can be planted in one pot.

4. Make sure the bulbs are placed not farther than 2 inches from the edges of the pot.

5. After watering through, put the pot in a cool location — around 60 degrees — and watch for the bulbs to produce shoots 4 to 6 inches long.

6. Move the plants to a sunny location and provide a balanced, full-strength fertilizer once a week.

7. Provide even moisture levels, but do not let the soil become too soggy because bulbs rot easily.

Air Layering

Air layering, rooting from a notch in the parent stem, is a propagation technique best suited for plants with woody stems, such as the *Dieffenbachia*, *Schefflera*, and *Dracaena* species. As these woody plants mature, their stems become long and lanky, and they tend to lose leaves at the base of the stem. The idea behind air layering is the parent plant continues to provide the appropriate water and nutrients to the new plant while it is establishing its roots. A benefit to this technique is that it does not require daily maintenance.

Steps for propagating by air layering

1. Use a sharp knife to cut the lower leaves on the main stem. Cut diagonally and partially through the stem. Make the cut directly below a leaf node.

2. Make a notch in the stem and remove a sliver of growth.

3. Using a toothpick or small, clean paintbrush, dust the notch with rooting hormone powder.

4. Wrap a plastic bag around the stem and fill it with dampened sphagnum moss.

5. Close the top of the bag with electrical tape or a twist tie.

6. Check weekly for moistness or to add more water as needed.

7. After roots develop, cut the stem of the plant below the plastic bag and remove the bag and the moss.

8. The new plant should be ready to plant in a new pot.

Chapter 10

Protecting Your Plants From Pests and Diseases

Your plants will give you clear signs when something goes wrong. If you are regularly caring for your plants, shifting them in the sun, and watering them as they need it, you will become familiar with the look of a healthy plant versus an ailing one. When a plant grows poorly, there can be a variety of causes. By following the information in this book on atmosphere, humidity, watering, and sunlight, you can eliminate environment as a problem. If you follow the advice on proper containers, soils, and nutrients, you will be assured that you are doing all you can to give your plants the right growing medium. At this point, it is time to check your sick plants for harmful insects and diseases.

Common Plant Pests

Indoor plants are susceptible to insects just as outdoor plants can be. Insects often love the stable atmosphere of a home and the absence of enemies, so they can freely propagate unless you take action to destroy them. They can enter your home from new plants or infested cuttings, or they can hitch a ride from the outdoors and nest in your plants. If you leave your plants outside in the summer and bring them inside in the fall, the pots might contain outdoor bugs like earwigs, ladybugs, or earthworms. The best practice is to quarantine a new plant in a different room and watch it for evidence of bugs or disease before allowing it to mix with other plants.

When one plant is infested, the pests can spread to nearby plants. However, some bugs prefer one type of plant and most likely will not bother adjacent plants. Some pests will burrow in the soil and damage roots, while others attack leaves, stems, or flowers. If you catch the infestation early enough, you will be able to save the plant, so inspect your plants as you water and care for them to prevent any problems before they cause too much damage. A plant that has sustained injury to more than half of its leaves and stems will not recover, but you might be able to take a fairly healthy cutting and start a new plant — *see Chapter 9 for instructions.*

An entire chemical industry has been founded on the prevention and destruction of plant diseases and harmful insects. You are likely to find remedies for any plant problem at your local garden center or greenhouse. It is important to be sure the insecticide label lists the insect you are trying to control. Use caution; not all treatments are safe on every houseplant; some plants are sensitive to any chemicals. Always follow the directions on the label and treat the plants in an area with good ventilation.

There are also many natural home remedies that work just as well, often with fewer harmful side effects than chemical treatments. It is always best to begin treatment with the gentlest remedy and move on to more aggressive methods if needed.

The following are complete descriptions of common bugs that harm houseplants and the treatments that will help destroy those pests. If your treatments do not resolve the problem, check with your local college extension office for additional ideas.

Two Natural Pest Remedies

1. If the plant is heavily infested, clean all sides of each leaf and stem in a lukewarm shower, or take the plant outside and spray it with a hose. Because some insects still cling to leaf crevices or stems, repeat the process a few days later.

2. For stubborn pests, use a soap rinse. First, wrap the pot in a plastic bag. Then, fill a sink with a solution of 1 teaspoon of mild dish soap to 1 quart of water. Swish the plant slowly and gently in the water for about a minute, making sure every part of the plant above the root crown makes contact with the soapy solution. Allow the plant to dry, out of contact with direct sunlight. Repeat this process several days later.

Aphids

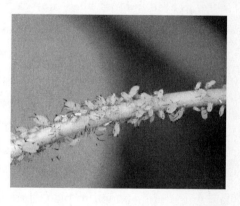

There are many types of aphids, but the one you will see most often in a houseplant is the green peach aphid. These insects are fairly indiscriminate in their tastes and could set up a home on just about any houseplants. Aphids are round or oval and range in color from green to yellow to red. They are large enough to see with the naked eye, being about $\frac{1}{12}$ inch long. Some of these insects have wings.

If you see one aphid, there are many more because these bugs live in colonies and reproduce rapidly. Aphids suck plant juices, preferring the tender leaves of new shoots or buds, or the tissues of weak plants. While sucking the juice from the plant's veins, they inject a poison that damages the plant even further. Plants that host aphids will have curled and distorted leaf tips and buds. Because aphids feed in dense groups and are fairly easy to see, just checking the undersides of leaves or the folds of buds will allow you to diagnose the problem.

It is fairly easy to rid a plant of aphids. If only a few leaves have colonies, you can just remove those leaves and discard them outside. For heavier infestations, try the lukewarm shower or soap rinse, making sure you repeat it a few days later to remove any stubborn insects. Alternatively, you can buy an all-purpose houseplant insecticide, and use it according to the directions. Make sure that you also wipe your windowsill with soapy water to ensure no aphids have been left behind.

Earwigs

Earwigs head indoors when the weather turns cold or hide in the bottom of planters that have spent the summer outside. You will recognize them by their reddish brown to black coloring. They are 9 to 15 millimeters long, have short wings near their head, and pincers at the back of their body. Even though the pincers of these bugs look vicious, they are not strong enough to pierce human skin.
Moreover, despite their name, they do not crawl into the ears of mammals and cause damage.

These pests are not a specific threat to plants, but they will eat leaves and roots if no other food can be found. Obviously, they are not desirable in the home. Earwigs like dark, damp places, so by uncovering these places you can catch them and deposit them outside, in the trash, or flush them down the toilet. You can also catch earwigs on standard sticky glue bug traps such as those used for ants, fleas, silverfish, or roaches. Follow manufacturers' directions for placement and warnings.

Earwigs do not reproduce inside the house. The dry air conditions inside prohibit reproduction. They can simply be removed and disposed of outside.

Fungus gnat

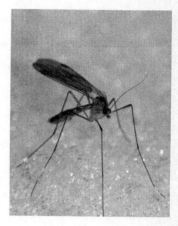

These insects are narrow, dark gray flying bugs about $\frac{1}{15}$ to $\frac{1}{20}$ inch long, though some are much smaller. You can see them moving around the soil in your plants, but they also flit around sources of heat and light like sunny windows or light bulbs. These insects can fly indoors through an open door and breed in houseplant soil.

Fungus gnats love a damp environment, so the insects are most prevalent when the soil is kept too moist. The adult fungus gnat can lay hundreds of eggs at a time, and when they hatch, out come the small white larvae. The larvae eat fungi growing on organic matter in the soil, but they can also feed on the plant's roots. You will be able to see the tiny, threadlike maggots wriggling at the surface of the soil when you water the plant. The larvae mature into adult flying pests in about two weeks, and easily migrate to other plants. If your plant is infested with fungus gnats, it will become weak, grow spindly stems, and start to drop older leaves.

The first step to eliminating these pests is to allow the soil of each infected plant to dry completely before watering again. A dried plant will deprive the gnats of their moist environment; however, if your plant is weak, it will be too harmful. You can also create a gnat-catcher with a piece of paper smeared with petroleum jelly or honey, staked into the soil or around light bulbs — the flies will stick to the paper and die. An old folk remedy is to put a slice of peeled potato on the surface of the soil. The larvae will burrow into the potato and can be removed every few days. You can also remove the plant from its pot and repot it in a clean container with new soil.

If none of these remedies work, there are commercial applications that will help. One is a solution of pyrethrum, a natural insecticide made from plants in the chrysanthemum/daisy family. Follow label directions for use, and be cautious; pyrethrum can be irritating to plants and your own skin. Commercial greenhouses also use a biological preparation, a strain of bacillus bacteria that kills larvae. Follow the directions to drench the soil and interrupt the breeding life cycle.

To prevent outbreaks in the future, clear away dead leaves and other organic matter from the surface of the soil. Make sure you do not overwater your plants, and keep an eye on the humidity level of the plant's windowsill.

Mealybugs

Mealybugs are similar to scale insects, and cause similar damage. These insects are ⅛ inch, pink or light brown pests that suck plant juices and introduce toxins to the plant's circulation. The affected stems and leaves will turn yellow and become weak. Mealybugs thrive in a warm, dry environment.

These insects can often be found in colonies at the root crown, on the undersides of leaves, or in the crevice between the leaves and petioles. They often produce a white, cottony patch on the stems, leaves, and roots. This coating can protect them from insecticides and water sprays, so it is most effective to remove them manually. You can pick them off the leaves with tweezers, wipe them off with a soapy rag, or use a cotton swab dipped in hydrogen peroxide to swipe them off the plant. Repeat this process once a week until no more bugs can be found. Spraying them with an insecticidal soap before manually removing the bugs will kill off a large portion of the population, leaving you with the task of killing any resistant bugs.

Nematodes

Stem and leaf nematodes are nearly transparent larvae that infest most soils. These microscopic worms can range in size from 0.3 millimeters to over 8 meters. Most of these nematodes are harmless to plants, but a few are parasites that attack the roots or the leafy parts of plants. Like most other pests, they suck sap from the plant and introduce poison into the plant's veins. An affected plant will show signs of leaf or root rot, developing a sour odor and drooping, damp foliage that is browning or blackening.

Nematodes require moisture to swim through the soil, so a main cause of damage is overwatered soil or water transferred from an affected plant to a healthy plant. If you allow the soil to dry fully, you will decimate the nematode population because a handful of soil can contain thousands of nematodes. But using a commercial pesticide designed to kill harmful nematodes will hasten their destruction.

Springtails

Springtails are tiny white or grayish, wingless bugs that look like flies. They get their name from the jumping action you can observe when you water a plant — they will flip around the soil and leaves. These pests like an environment of moist

soil and plenty of algae, fungi, or rotted plant matter to feast on, but they are rarely a danger to the plant itself.

To rid your plant of these bugs, try allowing the plant to completely dry out before watering again. This procedure will kill most of the pests. You can also try removing the plant from the pot and removing as much soil as possible from the root ball. Then submerge the root ball in water for several hours. A drenched root ball will drive all the springtails out of the plant. Be sure to thoroughly clean the pot and then add fresh soil when re-planting. The old soil can be discarded outside.

Scale

Scale insects are whitish brown or tan in color and are slightly raised from the surface of the plant in miniature bumps that look like caps or helmets. New larvae are too small to be seen without a magnifying glass.

Scale insects often attach to plants that have been transplanted or cultivated from outside. Scales can be found on plant parts above and below the soil. Even if you treat the plants before bringing them inside, the scales can be under the soil and continue to survive. They will eventually go above the soil line on the plant and attach to the leaves and stems. Scales are not fussy about which plants they choose; just about any plant will satisfy them. For this reason, if you see one plant with scales, check all your plants for problems.

These insects spend much of their life cycle under a shell they extrude when young, which protects them and keeps them from drying out. Each scale insect can produce hundreds of young under the protective shell. These pests also suck the sap from plant veins.

Because the protective coating is difficult to penetrate with treatments, try to catch the insects before they develop their shells, and rinse them off with a sprayer or lukewarm shower. Most signs of infestation appear only after the insects have firmly attached to the plant. You should be able to spot the scale bumps on the undersides of the plants.

Using the soap rinse solution described above, wet a cloth and try to wipe the scales off the plant. Then treat the plant with a commercial insecticide soap or horticultural oil and place it out of the sun until dry. For more persistent problems, there are numerous aerosol and pump spray treatments as well as insecticidal soaps available to treat these insects. Unlike other houseplant insects, you will have to repeat treatments for scales three to four times to be sure you have controlled all the larvae and adults.

Spider mites

Spider mites are one of the most common household pests. They thrive in a hot, dry climate, so they are particularly prevalent indoors in winter. These pests, classified as part of the arachnid family, are tiny and are barely visible to the naked eye. They range in colors from red, brown, green, or yellow and are oval-shaped. Magnification is often required to see them. One common detection method is to shake or tap leaves over a white cloth or white paper to see if particles are moving. The red spider mites are easiest to detect using this method.

These pests can severely damage windowsill plants by removing sap and chlorophyll, primarily feeding on the underside of leaves. The underside of the leaves is where the spider mites congregate. In larger infestations, you can spot a spider web-like coating on the underside of the leaves and near the stems. Spider mites can spread to other plants on the sill. You will see small yellow spots from where they have been feeding, or in severe cases, yellowed or brown leaves that hang limp. The leaves can appear pale because the chlorophyll is being removed. Spider mites can reproduce rapidly, with a complete life cycle of less than two weeks. Eggs will hatch in as little as three days. If humidity is increased, this life cycle can be reduced or stopped altogether.

Controlling spider mites is difficult, but not impossible. Because they like a dry, warm environment, it is good to increase the humidity in the house or mist the plants regularly. The increased humidity will slow the spread of the mites. Isolate infected plants whenever possible. Be sure to wash the windowsill with soapy water after removing infested plants to remove any remaining bugs. If it will not severely damage the plant, remove the infested leaves and carefully dispose of them. Spray the plant with water to help physically remove the spider mites and silky webbing. Treat plants by spraying with insecticidal soap. Some insecticides are commercially available, but check with your local extension office for products that are legal to use in your state. One problem with the use of insecticides is the possibility spider mites will build up a resistance. A basic oil/soap mixture can be effective for control. Mix and use the following simple solution to spray the underside of the infected plants two to three times, five days apart:

2 tablespoon vegetable oil

1 tablespoon mild dishwashing liquid soap

2 quarts warm water

Thrips

These are small, slim insects that
are difficult to see without magnification. They are dark or tan-
colored as mature adults with tiny,
wispy wings. In the larval stage,
they are pale yellow or white without wings. In both stages, they look

like small bits of thread. Thrips are more common on outdoor plants
than on indoor plants. They often come inside with plants kept outside
in the summer and brought inside for the winter. The adults can jump,
scurry away, or fly when disturbed.

Thrips feed on the leaves and flowers of windowsill plants. They use their
jagged mouths to scrape the surface of the leaf or flower to suck out nutrients. These feeding strips appear as whitish streaks or pale spots. Sometimes there will be tiny black spots of black excrement on the leaves and
streaks or discoloration on the flowers. Severe damage is evident in curled,
streaked leaves.

To control thrips, start by pruning the infected leaves. Then wash the
plants outside or in the shower. Pruning the leaves will physically remove
the insects. Insecticidal soaps can be sprayed on the infected plants five
days apart for two to four treatments. Commercial insecticides can be effective. Check with your local extension office for available insecticides in
your state.

Whiteflies

These are small, gnat-like insects that look like small moths with four wings. They are related to aphids, scales, and mealybugs. They are easy to spot, especially when you are watering or moving your plant as they will fly off it. You can easily see these whiteflies swarming around the plant.

Whiteflies, especially the flat whitefly larvae, damage the plants by sucking the sap and juices from the leaves. The leaves will go pale yellow and hang limply or fall off. Often, they will take in more juices than are digestible, resulting in the excrement of a sticky substance referred to as honeydew. Black, sooty mold can grow on this excrement, which can then restrict the photosynthesis of the plant and further stunt plant growth. The honeydew can also be attractive to other pests.

To control whiteflies, begin with a mechanical removal by spraying or showering the plant. Remove damaged, infested leaves and safely dispose of them. Before using harsher treatments, try spraying the plants with insecticidal soap every five days. Tender, more sensitive plants can be sprayed with an equal mixture of water and rubbing alcohol. Treat with this mixture every seven to eight days. Commercial insecticides such as pyrethrin or similar compounds can be sprayed as directed on the label. It is a good idea to use a sticky glue trap following treatment to attract and capture remaining adult whiteflies.

Common Plant Diseases

Many plant diseases are caused by mold or other fungi. Indoor windowsill plants have less of a problem with most plant diseases than outdoor plants. The protected environment indoors helps eliminate many of the sources for plant diseases, such as dampness, insects, and harsh conditions. These conditions cause more stress to plants, making them susceptible to many types of diseases. Diagnosing disease causes in indoor plants is difficult because of the common symptoms with insect infestation. It is important to carefully diagnose the problem and be certain the right treatment regime is being utilized. Another challenge that arises is that one problem can serve as the catalyst for others. For example, damage from whiteflies can lead to sooty mold.

Mold

Molds are types of fungi found in the soil and on dead decaying material. Mold can develop on the topsoil of indoor plants. They come in a variety of colors, such as black, white, green, brown, and even orange. Molds naturally occur in the environment and have a musty or earthy odor to them. Similar to plants that produce seeds, molds make tiny spores to reproduce. When allowed to rest in a damp spot, molds begin to grow and multiply.

Mold can develop on the surface of the soil on your plants. When you see this, scrape off the moldy soil 1 to 2 inches deep, making certain not to damage the plant's roots. Add some fresh all-purpose potting soil to the top of the pot. Using soilless potting soil will help control new growth because it is sterile. Water the plant thoroughly so that the new soil can blend in. As an organic remedy, sprinkle the top of the soil with ground cinnamon. Cinnamon has some natural fungicidal characteristics. If this does not control the mold, try using a commercially available fungicide. The problem with using a fungicide, however, is that it functions better as preventative measure rather than as a cure. Fungicides also work better in outdoor conditions. It is best to control the environment to prevent mold growth.

Gray mold

Botrytis blight, or gray mold, is rare on indoor plants because of the controlled, dry environment. It is most common outdoors and can be a problem in greenhouse conditions. The fungus *Botrytis* is the cause of gray mold and grows on stems, leaves, and flowers. Severely infected plant parts will become brown or black and eventually die. Remove any infected parts and dispose of carefully. The best prevention is providing a healthy environment with good air circulation and balanced humidity depending on the season, as well as keeping leaves dry.

Powdery mildew

Powdery mildew is a more common problem outdoors but can occasionally occur on windowsill plants. The common symptom is the white, powdery growth on plant leaves. You can also get brown spots that are thin and paper-like. Powdery mildew is caused by two species of the *Oidium* fungus. It is transmitted from plants that come inside from outdoors. The mildew spreads by spores. The spores are blown in the wind or drafts to other parts of the plant. The spores can also live in the soil or in dead plant material. Powdery mildew thrives in warm, humid environments, so it does not survive well in the dry air inside. The best cure is to remove the infected leaves and dispose of them carefully so spores are not spread to other plants. Also be certain there is good air circulation and ventilation. Be careful to not overwater plants as the humid environment encourages mildew growth.

Root rot

Root rot, and the related stem rot, can be the most prevalent disease problem in windowsill plants. Root rot is caused by a variety of fungi that can lay dormant in the soil. Overwatering also contributes to the growth of the fungi responsible for root rot. The symptoms are brown or black plant tissue at the base of the plant above or below the soil line. Leaves and stems will begin to hang limp and curl up in more severe cases. The best bet for treating is to remove the affected roots and stems, gently wash the plant, and then repot it. Always use a sterile pot and soilless potting mix, which is also sterilized. Some fungicides are available, but these might not be worth the cost.

Black sooty mold

Black sooty mold develops on the honeydew excreted by insects such as whiteflies. This mold is not particularly harmful to the plant, but it is dark and dense, so it can block the light from absorbing into the plant tissue. The best course of treatment is to use a damp cloth and remove the sooty mold. Focus your efforts on determining the insect infesting the plant and excreting the honeydew, and treat as indicated above.

Anthracnose disease

Anthracnose in houseplants is commonly caused by one of two fungi from the *Colletotrichum* or *Gloeosporium* family. When this disease is present, the leaves start turning yellow, then eventually dark brown around the edges and tips. Keep the air circulation good and humidity under control. Remove the infected leaves and dispose of them carefully to prevent further spread. Infected plants should be isolated until the problem comes under control.

Chapter 11

Continued Care for Your Plants

You have chosen the right soil, watered your plants as needed, placed them in the right windowsill, and monitored them for bugs and disease. Your plant will need only a few more points of care to keep it looking beautiful and healthy for years to come.

Periodically Check Your Plant's Soil

The plant's soil will need periodic attention. As mentioned in Chapter 7, salts can leach out of the soil over time. Even with careful fertilizing, the soil will eventually become used up and less fertile. One solution is to re-move the plant, shake the soil from the roots, discard the soil in the pot, and re-pot the plant with fresh soil. Moving the plant to a bigger pot pro-vides an excellent time to refresh the soil. However, if salts have accumu-lated at the edges of the pot, but the soil appears to be otherwise healthy, you may want to try top-dressing. Top-dressing entails digging away the first few inches of pot soil, depending on the pot size, and adding new, rich soil. Carefully mix the new soil with the layers below, without disturbing the roots if possible.

When Your Plant Has Gotten Too Big For Its Pot

Any well-nurtured and untrimmed plant will eventually outgrow its pot. If you have room for a larger plant on your windowsill, repot it to give it new life and healthier foliage. Plants overdue for repotting will be root-bound; the roots will fill the pot in a convoluted tangle that uses up most of the soil. Indications that your plant has outgrown its living space include:

- The roots are growing out of drainage holes.

- The roots are cracking the pot.

- The plant is top-heavy.

- The plant wilts within a day or two of watering.

- There is very little soil left in the container.

You have two options: 1) reduce the size of the plant, or 2) increase the size of the pot. If you have been clipping the plant back all along, the roots will keep pace with the foliage and will not overrun the pot. But when a plant becomes overgrown, you will have to trim back a third of the roots and foliage before replanting in the same pot with new soil. Knock off old soil if any remains and unwind any circling roots. Remove roots that look rotted or could use trimming. Water the plant well, and expect some dieback from leaves that were fed by the roots you trimmed away. The plant will take hold and begin to grow again within a month or two.

Allow the soil to dry somewhat before you try to repot it; this will make it easier to remove the plant while keeping the soil and roots intact. Follow these helpful hints to ensure successful removal without damaging the plant:

1. When removing the plant, do not yank on the stems or leaves. Instead, run a dull knife or spatula around the edge of the pot from

top to bottom to loosen the soil from the container.

2. Place your hand over the top of the pot with the foliage between your fingers.

3. Tap on the bottom of the pot a few times to loosen the plants.

4. Gently pull the plant out while continuing to tap.

If you choose instead to put your root-bound plant in a larger container, soak the root ball in water to make the roots looser and more flexible. Then use a fork or narrow stick to detangle the roots slightly. Pot the plant in new soil, making sure the roots have at least 1 inch of room around each side for growth. After transplanting, a plant needs a few weeks of rest before you will see any new growth.

Take Good Care of Those Leaves

Along with soil maintenance, you will need to perform leaf maintenance on most of your plants over time. Bromeliads that are fertilized through organic matter held in central leaf "water cups" should be rinsed out with distilled, contaminant-free water every few years. All plants, except desert species, should be given a shower two or three times a year to rinse off the leaves and stems. Desert plants can be rinsed once a year to remove dust and contaminants, especially debris that may collect in the spines. However, when you rinse these plants, either hold them sideways so you do not soak the soil with water, or wait until the plant is overdue for watering so that the plant does not get too much water at once.

Grooming Your Plants

Even the most experienced, green-thumbed gardener can make a gardening mistake that results in plant damage. Sometimes disease, lack of water, too much water, or contaminants may damage the foliage before you can take corrective action. After the problem is resolved, it is time to restore the beauty of the foliage. Plants such as the white flag will respond dramatically to a lack of water by first wilting, then developing brown leaf edges. You can use a pair of sharp, clean scissors to remove the brown leaf edges and maintain the green beauty of the plant. Similarly, you can remove dead leaves, stems, and debris from the plant and the topsoil to prevent disease and improve your plant's appearance.

You have already learned about clipping or trimming plants to keep them from overgrowing the pot. But gardeners may also choose to clip or trim plants for other reasons. Some plants, such as the coleus, will produce flower spikes that divert all the plant's resources to nurturing the flowers. The coleus plant is often grown for its astonishing multicolored foliage rather than the insignificant flower spikes, so you may want to pinch off or clip the flower spikes to encourage foliage growth. In many plants, the foliage will continue to grow in an upward pattern unless you snip off the tip. Pinching the top will encourage the plant to produce offshoots or side foliage that develops into a nicely shaped, bushy plant. If you notice a pleasing pattern in the foliage of a plant, you can encourage the shape through judicious trimming.

Occasionally, a woody plant or one growing with long central stems may begin to grow crookedly. In some cases, you can encourage even growth by changing the plant's orientation to the sun throughout the week. But some plants need a little help, just like a damaged bone needs a splint to help it grow straight again. You can use commercial plant stakes, wooden chopsticks, tall nails, toothpicks, or similar rigid objects as splints, according to the size of the plant. Press the stake into the soil, being careful to avoid piercing roots. Then attach the stake to the plant with twine, twist ties, rags, or other soft materials. Some plants will develop a straight stem and will eventually be hardy enough to grow without the stake. Other plants may need permanent strength from the makeshift splint.

Though you may feel like a plant seems to require a copious amount of care when you read these instructions, you will become familiar with your plant's needs over time. Becoming familiar with one type of plant may increase your desire for others. After living with a plant for a while, you will be able to see signs and anticipate the care a plant needs, just as you learn the needs and signs of people and pets in your home. In this way, a plant can become more than a decorative object; it can be another living organism for you to nurture.

Watering Plants While You Are Away

If you go away for an extended period of time, you will want to take a few precautions to ensure that your plants are properly cared for and will still be alive and healthy when you return. For short vacations of seven to ten days, begin by watering plants thoroughly, including wetting the foliage well. You can leave the plant in a saucer or drip pan in up to 1 inch of standing water. The plants will lose less moisture if you move them away from sunny windows into cooler areas of the house. In the winter, adjust the thermostat a few degrees lower before leaving; 60 to 65 degrees Fahrenheit is ideal. If you are away during the summer, it is wise to keep the air conditioner running to no higher than 80 to 85 degrees. However, if you plan to turn the air conditioning off during your vacation, place the windowsill plants in a room without heavy direct sun in which the temperature will be fairly cool and constant.

Garden stores and florists sell commercial products that can water plants automatically while you are away, and some can accommodate multiple plants at a time. Such products usually have a water reservoir and a tube or wick that channels water into the soil. As the plant uses moisture, it draws from the reservoir. There are other ways to ensure that your plants receive the proper water while you are away without spending money. Some of these methods are easy to create or arrange yourself.

- **Makeshift greenhouse** — Houseplants can thrive for up to three weeks while you are away if you fashion a makeshift greenhouse for them. After watering a plant, push wooden stakes into the soil. Cover the plant, pot and all, with a clear plastic bag. Make sure that the stakes keep the plastic from touching the foliage. Place the plant inside the bag and close off the bag with a rubber band or a twist tie. The plant will continue respiration, and the water will condense against the sides of the plastic and return to the soil. Also keep the plant away from direct sunlight. If your plants are large, wrap the plastic bag only around the pot itself, and seal the plastic around the bottom of the stems with yarn or twine. This environment will keep larger plants moist for seven to ten days.

- **Bathtub greenhouse** — You can also keep your plants happy and healthy while you are on vacation by turning your bathtub into a greenhouse. You can do this in several ways. One way is to line the bathtub with a plastic sheet and then set a layer of bricks in the tub. Fill the tub with water to the level of the bricks, and set plants on the bricks. Another method is to put thick layers of newspaper over the plastic sheet. Arrange the plants on top of the newspaper, close enough to touch each other and therefore conserve moisture. Pour water on the newspapers until they are thoroughly wet. Then close the shower curtain to keep the moisture inside the tub. When you leave, you can keep the bathroom light on and close the door.

- **Homemade watering system** — You can make a homemade watering system instead of buying one by using an empty soft drink or water bottle with a screw-top lid and a pair of nylon panty hose. A single-serving bottle works best for smaller plants; a 2-liter bottle will work for larger plants. With a pair of scissors, cut off the base of the bottle, then drill three or four tiny holes in the plastic cap. Cut a square of panty hose material and put it over the opening of the bottle. Fill the bottle with water and screw the cap on over the panty hose. The nylon will filter dirt away from the holes in the cap. Bury the cap and neck of the bottle in the dirt next to your plant. It should be buried deeply enough to remain upright and not tip over. Over time, the water will drip out of the bottle and into the soil.

- **Let gravity water your plants** — If you need to water several plants at a time, you can also make a device like those sold commercially at home with a large jar and cotton or polyester rope. Fill the jar full of water and place it higher than the level of the plants. Each section of rope should span the length from the bottom of the jar to each plant's pot. Put the rope down into the jar and put the other end on the soil surface of each plant. The water will draw down the length of the rope and slowly water the pots while you are gone.

- **Defer to the house sitter** — For trips longer than ten days, ask someone to care for your houseplants and any outdoor plantings. Give your caretaker clear directions and all the supplies they will need. For convenience, group all arid plants in one windowsill and keep the water-loving plants in another area, so there is no confusion on which plants need special care.

Conclusion

You now have the ability to select windowsill plants that can add life, beauty, fragrance, and functionality to your home year-round. Growing houseplants can be relatively simple when you have the proper background on the plant's growing habits and basic requirements. Beyond adequate light, water, and humidity, most windowsill plants require minimal care. Refer back to this guide frequently to ensure that you are providing optimal care for your plants. Once you have mastered a few plants, reference the plant profiles in chapters 2 through 5 to identify other plants you can add to your collection.

Whatever your taste, this guide provides a variety of common plants that can brighten your mood, freshen the air, add color to your décor, and improve the quality of the air in your home. With this book as your companion, you are well-equipped to create one, two, or several windowsill gardens throughout your home. And with the increasing motivation to go "green," what better way to begin than with living, breathing greenery?

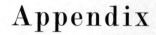

Appendix

Resources for Buying Plants and Seeds Online

You can find many reputable and customer-friendly resources for buying houseplants and seeds online. This list is not exhaustive, but as of the time of publishing, these companies are some of the best — offering both indoor and outdoor plants along with a wealth of information about the products they supply. Many of these businesses also have printed catalogs, which you can sign up to receive in the mail.

Spring Hill Nursery

www.springhillnursery.com
Spring Hill Nursery has been in business for about 150 years as a plant developer and supplier of many types of perennial plants. Their online store allows shoppers to take advantage of good prices on high-quality plants developed from their years of experience.

Breck's

www.brecks.com
Breck's offers quality bulbs and excellent service. They allow customers to order in advance, and when their bulbs are ready for shipping, their staff of Dutch bulb experts selects the best bulbs of the current crop to fill orders.

Dutch Gardens

www.dutchgardens.com

Dutch Gardens has been a premier Dutch bulb and plant company for over 50 years. They offer many familiar plants and unusual and rare specimens, and their plant experts provide help in growing their products at home.

Park Seed

www.parkseed.com

Park Seed Company has supplied high-quality seeds and expert service for over 100 years. Their website's store offers many varieties of flower and vegetable seeds, annual and perennial, as well as plants and bulbs. Park Seed also sells seed-starting supplies, tools, and gifts.

Thompson & Morgan

www.thompson-morgan.com

Thompson & Morgan has been around for over 150 years. Thompson & Morgan is a U.K.-based company that provides gardening supplies to countries worldwide. They are experts in the garden and offer a wide selection of seeds, plants, bulbs, and gardening equipment.

Wayside Gardens

www.waysidegardens.com

Wayside is another excellent supplier of plants, bulbs, and gardening tools. Their payment and replacement policies are top-notch, and their website offers excellent plant information.

Richters Herbs

www.richters.com

Based in Canada, this company offers an excellent variety of herb plants and seeds. They ship around the world and take special care to package products so that herb plants are delivered to your door safely.

1-800-FLOWERS.COM

www.1800flowers.com

This site is not just for sending floral bouquets to your loved ones. They have an extensive collection of plants suitable for indoors, including flowering plants, fragrant plants, and bonsai plants.

Online Resources for Houseplant Gardeners

The Internet is a wonderful tool for finding additional information about houseplant care and specific information about your plant varieties. You can join gardening forums to discuss and learn more about houseplants or read other gardeners' experiences. As of the publishing date of this book, the resources listed below are some of the best online sources of information. You can also check your state's extension office for helpful information.

The Royal Horticultural Society

www.rhs.org.uk

The Royal Horticultural Society is a British charity dedicated to promoting horticulture and providing resources and knowledge for good gardening. They aim to help people with a passion for gardening become more skilled in horticulture and encourage people who have an interest in gardening.

The National Gardening Association

www.garden.org

The National Gardening Association offers one of the Web's largest and most respected arrays of gardening content for consumers and educators, from general information and publications to lessons and grants.

National Agricultural Library

www.nal.usda.gov

One of four national libraries, the National Agricultural Library maintains a comprehensive collection of horticulture information. This library is also the hub of information for the U.S. Department of Agriculture's network of libraries and state land-grant libraries.

PlantCare.com

www.plantcare.com

This site offers information for the casual cultivator and gardening guru. It includes an extensive plant information database, discussion forums, gardening tips, and guides.

Scotts Miracle-Gro Company

www.scotts.com

A maker of houseplant fertilizers and soils, this company is an expert at ensuring the health of houseplants. Browse their website for excellent information on all aspects of houseplant care.

The Encyclopedia of Houseplants

www.gflora.com

Here you will find more than 300 various houseplants with descriptions, pictures, botanical and common names, and instructions for cultivation and propagation. This website also includes a "plant identificator" to help beginners identify a plant.

Some universities are noted for their agricultural programs and provide a wealth of online and print resources for gardeners. Some of the best universities for plant information include the University of Illinois, Michigan State University, Texas A&M, the University of Hawaii, Tuskegee University, the University of Arizona, the University of Florida, and Auburn University.

Many home improvement and chain houseplant providers and florists offer online and print resources for gardeners. Be sure to pick up these additional resources for houseplant gardeners.

Glossary

Adventitious root: A root that originates from a location other than underground; for example, growing out from a stem or leaf.

Air layering: A propagation technique used on woody-stemmed plants.

Alkaline: A non-acid substance that has a pH greater than 7.0.

Bonsai: A dwarf ornamental tree or bush grown in a shallow dish or tray.

Bud: A protrusion at the tip of the stem that develops into a flower.

Bulb: A fleshy underground root structure from which a flower plant develops.

Bulblet: A small, immature bulb formed at the base of a parent bulb, such as in the hyacinth.

Chelation: A process used to treat micronutrients to keep them readily available to the plant when introduced into the soil.

Corm: A solid underground storage root found at the base of a stem. Often mistaken for a bulb, rhizome, or tuber, corms are more dense and woody.

Cultivar: A unique or distinctive plant variety propagated from the mother plant to keep certain desirable traits. A shortened term made up of the words "cultivated variety."

Cutting: A propagation technique where the stem or leaf part of a plant is removed and repotted to start a new plant.

Deadheading: Removing dead flowers from a plant to encourage new growth and prevent seed production.

Division: A propagation technique used to divide a plant into two or more equal pieces that either uses a bud or roots from which to start a new plant.

Evergreen: A plant with foliage that remains green year-round.

Frond: A large leaf, especially in ferns, with many divisions.

Humus: Fibrous, decomposed organic matter in soil, which provides nutrients and facilitates drainage in potting media.

Hybrid: A plant resulting from cross-breeding parents of different varieties, species, or families.

Isolate: Keeping a pest-laden plant at least 10 feet away from other plants.

Leggy: Overly tall or elongated, in a plant, often as a result of insufficient light or lack of pruning.

Microclimate: A small, localized environment having a unique climate that varies from the larger surrounding climate.

Mist: To spray a plant with light water droplets to clean the foliage and increase the humidity.

Offsets: When a plant produces young plantlets from the main or "mother" plant.

Ovule: A small seed plant structure containing the embryo sac and surrounded by the nucleus.

Peat: A type of soil containing partially decayed mosses and sedges from wet, boggy areas. It is used to soil texture.

Peaty: Resembling the taste and smell of peat.

Perlite: Volcanic glass used in potting mixtures to create space for air circulation.

Pest: An insect or animal that can threaten the health and well-being of a plant.

Petiole: A thick leaf vein that attaches to the leaf stem and looks similar to a stalk.

pH: The measure of the acidity or alkalinity of a solution, numerically equal to 7.0 for neutral solutions, increasing with increasing alkalinity and decreasing with increasing acidity. The pH scale ranges from 0.0 to 14.0.

Photosynthesis: A process that combines sunlight, water, and carbon dioxide to produce oxygen and sugar as food and energy for a plant.

Pinching: Removing soft growing tips of plants with your fingers to encourage bushy growth.

Potash: Chemically, a mixture containing potassium carbonate or potassium chloride.

Potting mix: A mixture or blend of soils used for container plants.

Propagate: The process of creating more plants from the primary plant.

Repotting: Moving a growing plant from one pot to a larger one to ensure further growth.

Rhizome: A storage root developing from a modified stem with several nodes that can produce either new stems or roots.

Root-bound: A term used for plants that have grown for too long in one container. The roots become intertwined, matted, and grow in circles because they have nowhere to spread. This can stunt a plant's growth.

Root rot: A soil-borne fungus caused by overwatering or poor soil drainage.

Rosette: New foliage coming out of a central cluster, often in a circular pattern.

Runners: Slender, trailing shoots emerging from a mature plant with new plantlets forming along the nodes of the shoots.

Seedling: A tiny new plant that grows from a seed.

Soilless: Refers to a potting medium containing a mixture of ingredients, but no mineral soil.

Spadix: A fleshy spike with numerous embedded small flowers.

Species: A group of plants sharing similar characteristics that can easily interbreed.

Sphagnum: A type of moss that grows in acidic conditions and is used for air layering or for lining hanging baskets.

Spore: The small, single-celled reproductive unit of many non-flowering plants.

Succulent: A plant that stores water in its stems, leaves, or thick roots, allowing it to thrive in arid climates.

Stolon: A modified stem that grows out from the parent plant and has buds capable of growing new plants.

Stomata: Pores in the leaves of plants that allow it to "breathe" by means of gas exchange.

Tendril: A threadlike part of a climbing plant, often in a spiral form, that supports the plant by clinging to or coiling around an object, such as a trellis or garden stake.

Terminal buds: Buds found at the end of a twig.

Top-dressing: Removing the first few inches of the soil and applying fresh new soil.

Transplant: The process of putting a plant in new soil or a larger container.

Tuber: A fleshy underground root or stem modified for food storage.

Variegated: Foliage with strikingly noticeable marbled, striped, patched, or blotched leaves.

Vermiculite: A naturally occurring mineral used in potting mixes that expands when heated. It is used to retain moisture and air within the soil.

Bibliography

Books

Bradley, Valerie. *The Complete Guide to Houseplants: The Easy Way to Choose and Grow Happy, Healthy Houseplants*. Reader's Digest, 2006.

Erler, Catriona Tudor. *Step-by-Step Successful Gardening: Herb Gardens*. Meredith Books, 1995.

Jantra, Ingrid and Ursula Kruger. *The Houseplant Encyclopedia*. Firefly Books, 1997.

Kramer, Jack. *Complete Houseplants*. Creative Homeowner, 2008.

Lehndorff, Betsy and Laura Peters. *Best Garden Plants for Colorado*. Lone Pine Publishing International, 2007.

Pleasant, Barbara. *The Complete Houseplant Survival Manual: Essential Know-How for Keeping (Not Killing!) More Than 160 Indoor Plants*. Storey Publishing, 2005.

Ortho: All About Houseplants. Meredith Books, 2007.

Ortho: Complete Guide to Houseplants. Meredith Books, 2004.

Websites

Custom Gardens, LLC. **http://customgardensllc.com**

Flowers Growing. **www.flowersgrowing.com**

Garden Chick. **http://gardenchick.com**

Garden Guides, Your Guide to Everything Gardening. **www.garden-guides.com**

Kemper Center for Home and Gardening. **www.mobot.org/gardeninghelp/plantinfo.shtml**

Mother Earth News. **www.motherearthnews.com**

Poisonous Plants of North Carolina. **www.ces.ncsu.edu/depts/hort/consumer/poison/poison.htm**

USDA Natural Resources Conservation Service, Plant Database. **http://plants.usda.gov**

You Grow Girl — Gardening for the People. **www.yougrowgirl.com**

Authors' Biographies

Donna M. Murphy is an editorial specialist, a seasoned writer, and a published author who has written, edited, and designed extensive collateral for print and the Web. She provides editorial and publication design services for industries such as information technology, entrepreneurial and business, and publishing and communications. Donna is the author of two non-fiction books: *Organize Your Books In 6 Easy Steps* and *A Woman's Guide to Self-Publishing*. She has also authored and published numerous resource booklets and has been featured in various magazines, business journals, and online communities, including *Real Women Real Issues, Work. Home.You, The Old Schoolhouse Magazine*, and *Bizymoms*.

Angela Williams Duea is a freelance writer and photographer who is passionate about food and gardening. She is president of Pearl Writing Services, which helps businesses communicate more effectively and helps individuals tell their stories. Angela lives in Chicago with her husband and has two daughters in college.

Index